# Lungeing and Long-Reining

# Lungeing and Long-Reining

JENNIE LORISTON-CLARKE, MBE, FBHS, NPS Dip.

KENILWORTH PRESS

First published in 1993 by
The Kenilworth Press Ltd
Addington
Buckingham
MK18 2JR

**British Library Cataloguing in Publication Data**
A catalogue record for this book is available from the
British Library.

ISBN 1 872 082 14 9


Photographs by Bob Langrish
Line drawings by Dianne Breeze
Design by Sandie Boccacci
Layout and typesetting by Kenilworth Press Ltd
Printed and bound by Hillman Printers, Frome

*To*

**Dutch Courage**

*who helped me to train horses in long reins
and who sired all the horses in this book.*

# CONTENTS

# Acknowledgements

I am grateful to Gyll Steele, who enabled me to progress in dressage by producing Kadett, my first Olympic ride, and then sharing Dutch Courage, who taught me so much.

I would also like to thank Sarah Whitmore and Hans Rochowansky who made all this possible by helping us to purchase Kadett and Dutch Courage, and especially 'Rocky' who taught me my initial in-hand work.

# Preface

When asked to write this book I felt rather diffident about the task as many successful trainers have written on the subject before. However, when I looked closely at what had been written it seemed to me that a great deal of knowledge and tips are passed on only by word of mouth from one's predecessors and these never reach the printed page.

It is for this reason - and the fact that I have been sent so many young horses who have been terrified by inept trainers and riders - that I have written this book.

Lungeing is an art and an excellent way of educating, exercising and suppling a horse. It helps both horse and handler to respect each other and also gives the rider a chance to see how the horse is moving and how his musculature and balance are improving with work, without the encumbrance of a rider.

There are many ways of educating horses and an open mind must be kept at all times. You can sometimes saddle up and mount a young unbroken horse all on the same day, but this won't educate his mouth nor his back muscles. You will therefore need, at some time, to lunge or long-rein your horse to help further his education. A horse that is correctly started should have a lovely mouth and be correctly balanced from the moment you start to ride him - and both can be achieved through lungeing and long-reining.

Later, when the basics have been firmly established, it is possible to introduce the horse to lateral work and even advanced movements such as tempi changes, piaffe and passage, all of which are described in this book.

The handler must, however, realise that a horse is a very powerful animal with extremely quick reactions. When frightened, a horse will usually run away; if cornered, he could kick with the hind legs, strike with the forelegs and/or bite with his teeth. When correctly handled and treated he usually becomes a very gentle, willing and obedient creature. This respect and willingness to please his handler is not obtained by feeding him titbits, but by giving him firm, clear orders which may have to be repeated many times. Praise and reward must be forthcoming as soon as the horse responds to a command. This should be given by a soothing voice and a stroke of the hand on his neck.

I make no apologies for repeating warnings about working in close proximity to horses during training sessions. **Never take chances.** Horses have kicked out at me on several occasions but the blows have never reached their target because I have been careful to concentrate on my horse and place myself at a safe distance when reprimanding him or asking him to do something he may not understand. Just because the photographs in this book show me working very close behind or to the side of my horse, it does not necessarily mean that you can or should do the same with your horse. Remember, I know my horses very well. Try to be aware of the dangers in lungeing and long-reining at all times.

I hope that by following the guidelines in this book you will be able to work towards greater harmony and friendship with your horse or pony, and on the way gain a greater awareness and understanding of that wonderful, most powerful, yet gentle and kindly animal - the horse.

# 1. Handling

When doing anything with animals, the first essential is to get to know each individual and assess his temperament, intelligence and attitude to work.

Fortunately, most horses are well handled from birth. They have been stabled, groomed and well cared for, and through their daily experiences have come to recognise man as a friend, a provider of food and an interesting companion who likes to fondle them. If correctly managed these horses are usually extremely easy to lunge and ride. However, like all creatures, if they learn any bad habits early on, and these are not recognised, there may well be bigger problems later, so faults must be corrected straight away.

Bear in mind the fact that a frightened horse usually runs *away* from the object of his fear. He will, in some cases, show his fear by kicking with his hind legs or striking out with his forefeet; also he could bite. Contact with any of these 'weapons' can be fatal or at least extremely uncomfortable! A horse is a very strong animal and these are his only forms of defence. So when handling horses it is important that you know what you are doing and have confidence in your actions. A person who nervously backs away from a horse is asking for trouble and the animal will sense this nervousness and could soon take to attacking the person. This animal is immediately classed as a rogue, but only because he has been incorrectly handled.

In a lifetime spent with horses I have met few truly savage horses, though many are talked about. I am sure that most behave in that fashion through incorrect handling; some because of tumours of the brain; and some because they are born disliking humans. I have once seen a foal who, when

first approached by man, has laid his ears back and looked very fierce, attempting to kick and bite. Foals like this need very careful early handling in the first weeks of life if they are to overcome this natural fear of man. Most foals, despite their timidity, will soon come up to explore this new 'object' in their presence. Some are keen to associate with man straight away.

## Safety

When working with horses there is a safety code that should be observed. These little tips are most important, which is why I have included them so early in the book:

♦ The horse should be taught to tie up.
♦ Never startle the horse; always talk to him when you are approaching or are about to enter his stable.
♦ Always put your hand on the horse's body before feeling his legs or head.
♦ Look the horse strongly in the eye when you need his attention or if he is to be corrected for something; look softly at him, not directly in the eye, if you need his trust and affection.
♦ Don't stand directly behind a horse until he can be trusted.

## Handling an untrained youngster

Today it is rare that you are sent a completely untouched three- or four-year-old for breaking, but it is not so unusual to meet an untrained, frightened horse or pony that has been chased off a transporter and into a stable and is simply scared out of his wits. How do you cope when every time you open the stable door, the horse cowers in the corner with his back to you, shaking in fright?

One way is to go very quietly into the stable with a little hay or oats and remain quite still in a corner. The idea is to allow the horse's own inquisitive nature to encourage him to come and investigate you. If you keep very still, and perhaps sit on a low stool so that you are not too tall, you become less awesome to him. Talk in a quiet and soothing voice and stay calm, still and relaxed when he eventually plucks up enough courage to sniff you out. In bad cases this could take several days, depending on the time you are prepared to give. Gradually the horse will come and talk to you and nuzzle your hair. This early, unforced contact with you is very important.

Little by little, as he becomes more bold you can begin to move your arms and perhaps touch his chin. You could also softly scratch his coat until be becomes confident that you are not going to hurt him. Soon you will be able to stand up and gently rub his shoulders and neck with your hand.

As you gain his trust you can quietly slip a rope over his neck and hold him steady while you put on a headcollar. This can be left on him in the stable, as long as it is correctly fitted and will not chafe the skin around the back of his jaw when he eats.

It is a good idea to plait a short rope about 30cm (1ft) long and leave it attached to the headcollar. This provides a useful 'handle' which you can hold whenever he comes up to you and use to hold him gently but firmly.

As his confidence grows so you will be able to teach him to tie up (which is dealt with in the next chapter) and learn to accept the touch of your hand all over his body. Once he is happy to let you caress him with your hands you can then start to use a soft brush or a cactus cloth or stable rubber.

Another way to begin to form a relationship with an untrained horse is to put him in an enclosed circular yard or pen, or a very large loose box, and with a short lunge rein advance towards him. When he shows interest in you, shake the rein at him, chase him away, then retreat and turn your back on him. After you have done this a few times he will realise that you are not hurting him. Continue chasing him around the yard (or box) in this way, and each time move away from him, and gradually he will start to come to you. It is as if he wants to ask you why you are doing this to him, and he wants to become your friend.

The next step is to put a headcollar on the horse, but don't expect him to be willing to allow you to do this straight away. First undo the nosepiece and attach the head band. Then, with one hand placed on the bridge of his nose, take the nosepiece over his nose and do it up loosely. Attach a short rope (about 30cm/1ft) to the headcollar and then leave the horse to think about his experience, stroking him on the neck as you leave him.

If you adopt either of the two approaches described above you will teach the horse always to come to you. With quiet, firm and just handling the horse will learn to accept you as his superior and a trusted friend.

Just like elephants, horses never forget, and a horse will 'tell' you exactly how he has been treated by humans. Anyone who has lost control of his temper with an animal should think seriously about continuing with the training of a horse. Other unsuitable candidates are those who take silly risks and don't think of the consequences.

# 2. Training the Young Horse

## Educating the foal and early leading

Ideally the training of a young horse should start from the day he is born. The foal should be gently handled and stroked on the neck and back. Your presence in the stable will make him familiar with you and he will learn not to be fearful of you. Very young foals can first be led beside their mother with a soft stable rubber around their neck and a hand behind their quarters. The latter will encourage them to go forward and stop them running backwards and possibly falling over. Such a fall should be avoided at all costs as a foal can be badly injured in this way.

*Fig. 1   Using a stable rubber for early leading of a foal.*

On about day three a foal slip can be placed on the foal. He can still be led beside his dam in the above way until he is quite familiar with the leading idea. Slight pressure on the lead rein and the hand behind the quarters will encourage him to come forward, and as soon as he does so the pressure must be slackened so that he receives a reward for the right reaction.

## Teaching to tie up

The early leading of the foal is important as it is the foundation for teaching him to tie up. This can be gradually taught while he is still with his dam, from two or three months onward. It is best carried out in a stable and it is important to have plenty of bedding, preferably shavings which don't slip as easily as straw.

The foal slip or headcollar needs to be strong so that it won't break if the foal pulls back hard on the rope. I like to start with a long rope, approximately 3.6m (12 feet) long, attached to a thick, well-fitting headcollar. I pass the rope through a ring on the stable wall and, holding it lightly, place myself towards the rear of the horse on either the near- or offside of his quarters.

If he does pull back I give him a smart flick with a cloth to drive him forwards so that he releases the tension on the rope. When he stands quietly without pulling back I reward him by speaking softly to him and giving him a stroke on the neck.

If you carry out this procedure every day and ask the foal to stand for five minutes tied in this way, he will soon learn what is required. You can

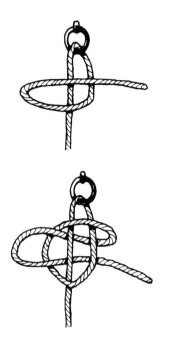

*Fig. 2   A quick-release knot should be used when tying up a horse. It can be undone quickly in an emergency.*

then progress to teaching him to stand tied when you are not in the stable. With this repetition and soft praise whenever he stands quietly, the foal will soon come to accept this form of discipline.

I always tie up my young horses directly to a secure tie-ring and not to a loop of string. The reason is simply that if the string breaks when the horse fights against it the horse will have learnt that he only has to pull back to free himself. However, the rope must be tied with a quick-release knot (see Fig. 2) so that you can untie it easily. It is also useful to have a thick rubber tie which is not so harsh as a rope, though you will still need a rope as a back-up.

If you have an older, fully grown horse who has not learnt to tie up, then be prepared to spend much longer on the learning process. When handling an unknown horse, then for safety reasons tie him up to a loop of string - if he panics, the string will break first.

Unfortunately there are many horses who have not been taught as foals or yearlings to accept being tied up, and these individuals are much more likely to put up a fight. However, time and patience usually win in the end.

## Grooming and handling

Now you can introduce him to grooming and get him used to a soft brush. Foals are very sensitive so a soft cactus cloth or stable rubber is often better than a brush in the early stages. If the horse is nervous his body will be tense and his senses magnified, so the kinder and more positive the touch, the easier it is for the horse to relax. The arm holding the cloth should therefore be used in a firm but relaxed manner.

When the horse becomes used to you handling him all over in this way and is confident because nothing has hurt him, you can introduce a soft body brush, preferably one with a leather back as these are not as rigid as the wooden-backed ones.

Sadly, I have seen many horses who have been made difficult to groom by thoughtless, rough handling in their early days. If a foal is ticklish and flicks up his feet, it is likely that some part of his body will get knocked by the back of the body brush. Obviously this will hurt him and he will become even more fidgety. Eventually he will start kicking and leaning towards you with one leg held up - and now you have the beginnings of a long-term behaviour problem.

It is important to realise that *any* brush is quite hard on a foal, and especially around the legs and under the belly where these youngsters are most sensitive. Do use all grooming tools with care.

The foal must learn to have his feet trimmed, so handling his limbs and teaching him to pick up his feet is very helpful for your farrier. A foal's feet should be regularly trimmed - every four to six weeks - and regular worming is needed after he is four weeks old.

At this point it is worth mentioning that too much human contact can have a detrimental effect on your relationship. Usually this is caused by people who think they should groom and pick out a foal's feet daily. Foals do get cheeky, but like all youngsters, their mother is the best person to sort them out, not us. However, if you are having to lead or groom a foal and he is naughty then he must have a sharp reprimand if he acts in any way which could become a dangerous habit. Rearing, kicking and biting are the most common sins, and whilst they don't worry you so much when witnessed in a sweet little foal, they are serious problems in fully grown horses. Your foal's mother will be quick to give him a sharp nip if he mistreats her - and you must respond equally quickly whenever his naughtiness involves you. All corrections must be **immediate** so that he associates his action with the correction.

## When to begin the training

When the foal is weaned he will either be fed in the field or he will come in every night for a meal. He will become accustomed to his daily routine, and provided he is fit and healthy, has his feet attended to and is wormed when necessary, there is no need to do anything more with him until he is a three-year-old. There is an awful temptation to lunge or long-rein a very young horse but I prefer to leave everything until they are three, or until at least four for a very large youngster. Of course,

thoroughbreds are bred to mature younger and are backed and ridden as early as two years old by lightweight riders.

If, however, you wish to show your yearling or two-year-old, then it is advisable to give him some early basic lungeing and leading lessons so that he shows himself off correctly and learns to stand. But if you do lunge any youngster it is important that it is only done on good going and in a large circle (see next chapter).

## Bits for very young horses

The bit you use on a young horse is important. The horse must be comfortable and learn to hold the bit correctly in his mouth.

Before even thinking of putting a bit in a horse's mouth I always check to make sure that he has no wolf teeth. These teeth are found in over sixty per cent of young horses and can cause a lot of discomfort when a bit is introduced. Wolf teeth are small, shallow-rooted teeth, usually found only in the upper jaw, just in front of the molars (see Fig. 3). They must not be confused with the tush of the male horse, which is much lower in the horse's mouth and very deep-rooted. If your horse has wolf teeth I recommend that you consult your vet-

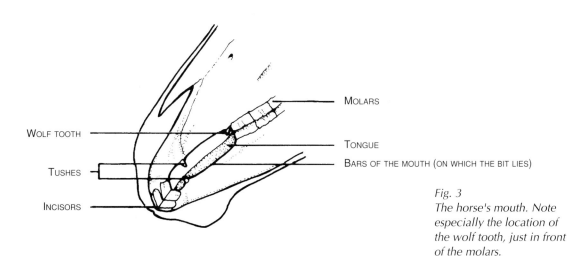

MOLARS

WOLF TOOTH

TONGUE

BARS OF THE MOUTH (ON WHICH THE BIT LIES)

TUSHES

INCISORS

*Fig. 3*
*The horse's mouth. Note*
*especially the location of*
*the wolf tooth, just in front*
*of the molars.*

*2.1   This straight-bar key bit is good for teaching a young horse to play with the bit so that he does not get a dry mouth - the more he uses his tongue, the more saliva he produces.*

erinary surgeon and have them removed before proceeding with the horse's education.

A young horse can have a bit introduced at an early age, even at six months in the case of a very big foal who needs to be controlled. At this age you could choose a very light nylon in-hand bit, a small rubber snaffle, or a mouthing bit with keys. This latter is designed to encourage the horse to use his tongue to play with the bit, and by so doing he creates plenty of saliva in his mouth.

The straight-bar key bit shown in Photo 2.1 should only be used as an introduction to bitting and not as a bit to ride with. You could also use a jointed key bit, but these are apt to hang too low in the horse's mouth. You *can* ride a horse in this latter bit but I have never found it necessary.

## Early lessons in leading

When leading a young horse in a bit, the lead rein can be attached to a coupling fitted to the nose-band of the headcollar or bridle so that there is not too much pressure put on the horse's mouth (see Fig. 4(a)). Rough handling now could damage the bars of the mouth and result in the horse having an insensitive mouth in later life.

When leading a horse the handler should always 'carry' his leading hand (more often the right hand as it is traditional to lead a horse from the near (horse's left) side).

Sometimes people lead horses with the weight of their arm pulling on the rein and dragging down the horse's head, which is wrong. The hand should

have a light feel on the rein, just as you would wish to have when riding the horse.

It is good practice to teach all young horses to lead from both sides. This prevents the horse from being one-sided in his physique, because when you are leading a horse he tends to bend slightly towards his handler.

When leading, do not allow the horse to turn his head away from you. If he does, you quickly lose control and he can easily trip you up with his front feet or can turn and kick you.

When teaching a horse to lead from the off-side the handler can either have an assistant walking behind the horse to encourage the animal to walk up beside the handler, or he (the handler) can carry a long whip that he can use to touch the horse behind to persuade him to keep up. The use of the voice at this early stage is essential. *'Walk on'* and *'whoa'* are good words to use.

*Fig. 4(a)   When leading a young horse in a bridle, the lead rein can be attached to the coupling and run through the back of the noseband so that pressure on the horse's mouth is regulated by the noseband.*

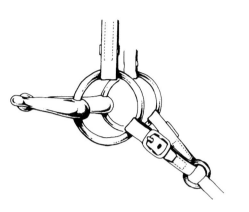

*Fig. 4(b)   A coupling strap attached to the bit rings avoids uneven pressure on the horse's mouth when leading in a bit.*

## Suitable bits for early training

When starting to educate a horse for lungeing and riding I prefer a lightweight **loose-ring snaffle** (see Photo 2.2). It has a thick, comfortable mouthpiece and is light and easily held up in the horse's mouth. It is also similar to the bridoon snaffle which the horse will meet when you introduce him to a double bridle later in his education. It is a bit which suits most horses and one I find very useful if a horse has an unsteady head-carriage.

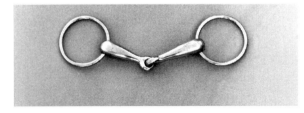

*2.2   A lightweight loose-ring snaffle. This bit is just what is says - light to hold in the horse's mouth. It is quite thick in diameter and nicely rounded in shape. If too narrow, it could pinch the corners of the mouth where the rings run into the bit, but when of the correct size it is the bit that most horses prefer.*

The **German hollow-mouth** loose-ring snaffle (shown in Photo 2.3) is heavier in weight and a little thicker in the mouthpiece. It is sometimes useful for a horse who is shy of taking a contact.

*2.3   The German hollow-mouth loose-ring snaffle is similar to the bit shown in Photo 2.2, but the mouthpiece is thicker throughout its length and it is quite a lot heavier in weight. It is a mild bit.*

The **unjointed rubber bit** shown in Photo 2.4 is soft and pliable and a lot of people like to start their horses with this bit. I have found that many horses hold this bit very still in the mouth and therefore seem to have a somewhat 'dry' mouth, which is undesirable. It is useful if you are leading a young horse and have to bit him for reasons of control. Being soft, the bit is unlikely to damage the horse's mouth should the horse get over-excited and leap around. Other similar bits are the vulcanite snaffle and the nylon in-hand bit. Like the key bit they are sometimes useful as an introduction to more 'grown-up' bits.

*2.4   Unjointed loose-ring rubber snaffle.*

The two cheeked snaffles in Photos 2.5 and 2.6 are useful bits and a popular choice when breaking and riding horses. The **Fulmer snaffle** is a heavy bit with a thick mouthpiece and is chosen for horses who are shy of the contact. The bit

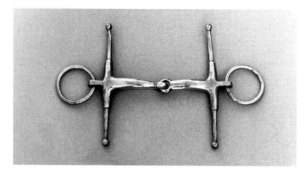

*2.5  A Fulmer snaffle.*

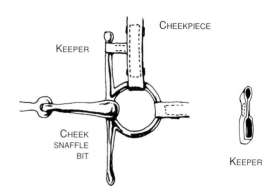

*Fig. 5  Cheek snaffle fitted with keeper.*

should be fitted with keepers as shown in Fig. 5. These keep the mouthpiece horizontal in the horse's mouth, and the cheeks prevent any likelihood of the bit pulling through the horse's mouth.

The **French-link cheek snaffle** (also shown in Photo 2.6) has a spatula mouthpiece making it double-jointed. It is similar to the Fulmer, but the nutcracker action is minimised due to the double joint and the fact that the ring and the cheek are co-joined. Like the Fulmer, this bit should be fitted with keepers.

The **French-link loose-ring snaffle** (see Photo 2.7) is used for horses who like a bit with a little more tongue pressure. Many horses favour this bit and the **hanging cheek snaffle** (Photo 2.8), which can also be obtained with a double joint and can be used with a double bridle. The hanging cheek bit tends to lie horizontally in the horse's mouth.

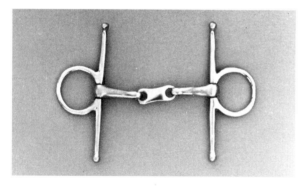

*2.6  A French-link cheek snaffle.*

*2.8  Hanging cheek snaffle.*

The **D-ring rubber-covered jointed snaffle** in Photo 2.9 is thought by some to be good for young horses. Its major disadvantage is that it falls low in the horse's mouth and only sits correctly across the mouth when considerable pressure is applied. I

*2.7  French-link loose-ring snaffle.*

*2.9  D-ring rubber-covered jointed snaffle.*

consider it a useful racing bit but not one for training young horses. I have had to train a number of horses who have been started with this bit and most have had tongue problems.

An **eggbutt snaffle** (see Photo 2.10) with a thick mouthpiece is a kind bit as it cannot pinch the corners of the mouth. However, because of the design of the ring it is inclined to hang a little low in the mouth. It is a very useful bit and also adapts to the double bridle easily.

There are other types of snaffle which can be used in early training but there is no need to look for complications. Try to keep everything as simple as possible so that when your horse is ridden he

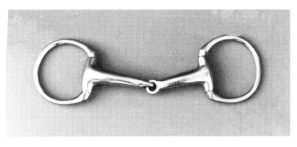

2.10   An eggbutt snaffle.

will not need to change to a very different bit. This is why I prefer the loose-ring lightweight snaffle or the eggbutt.

# 3. Lungeing

Lungeing is a way of exercising horses. It is also a means of training a young horse and of teaching it the aids of the voice, whip and rein. Once a horse has learned to lunge correctly, he can then be exercised safely in a field or at a show. A horse who has never been educated in this way can only be exercised by allowing him to run loose in a field or purpose-built area, or by riding him. There are many different ways that lungeing and long-reining can help in the education of the horse.

When lungeing the horse, he is controlled by a lunge rein attached to a cavesson. A lunge whip is employed to encourage forward movement, and the handler's position in relation to the horse can further promote forward activity or a decrease of pace. The voice is used to create impulsion and forward movement, to soothe and decrease the pace, to give directions, and to reward.

## Equipment

- Lungeing cavesson. There are various types: leather with one ring - suitable for lungeing for exercise; leather or nylon with three rings - suitable for lungeing and for use with side-reins attached; and the Wells cavesson which is more severe as it is fitted a little lower on the nose and fastened as a drop noseband, with the straps coming below the bit (see Photo 3.3). Note: some horses dislike the weight of a cavesson and are best started with a simple, strong head-collar.
- Lunge rein. These are made of linen webbing or cotton and should be 35mm (1.5 inches) thick and 7.2m (24ft) long. At one end they have a swivel and buckle strap fastening, or a swivel with spring-hook fastening.
- Lunge whip. This should preferably be 2.5m (about 8ft) long with a 2m (6ft) lash. I prefer the lash to be a continuation of the whip rather than a separate attachment.
- Four brushing boots for leg protection
- Snaffle bridle (optional)
- Gloves for the handler
- An assistant - depending on the ability of the lunger

You will also need access to a suitable lungeing area. A purpose-built circular lungeing ring is ideal; if not available, use an indoor school or corner of a small paddock. The lungeing area should be self-contained, if necessary separated off with jump stands, poles and/or straw bales. It should be sited away from distractions otherwise the young horse will find it difficult to concentrate.

The diameter of the lungeing area should be 15-20m (16-21yds); it should be level and with good footing. A grass area is only acceptable for a short time as it soon becomes rutted and poached and/or hard and slippery. Good footing is essential if your horse is to be able to concentrate and balance himself correctly. A sand and shavings or sand and fibre mix are the most suitable surfaces on which to lunge as they don't slip and are soft in all weathers.

## Fitting the lungeing cavesson

A lungeing cavesson is a strong, adjustable head-

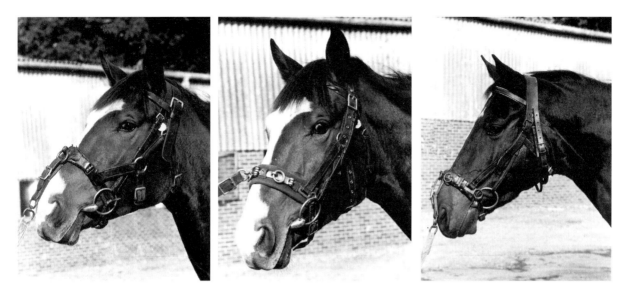

3.1   A single-ring cavesson with three straps under the jaw. Note that the cheekpieces of the bridle come outside the cavesson nose- band to allow the bit to move freely.

3.2   This nylon three-ringed caves- son has only two straps under the jaw, so both must be secured firmly or the cheekpiece could be pulled too near the horse's outside eye during lungeing.

3.3   A Wells cavesson with three rings and three straps.

collar of leather or nylon with a padded, hinged, metal ·nosepiece. Fitted to the front of the nose- piece are one or three rings to which you can attach the lunge rein (Photos 3.1-3.2).

The **normal cavesson** (shown in Photo 3.2) is fitted like a headcollar, with the headpiece coming just behind the ears. The noseband is fitted just below the cheekbones. If the cavesson has three straps, the throatlash is done up quite loosely so that you can fit your fist between the strap and the horse's throat. The cheek strap should be fastened firmly to prevent the cheekpieces moving near the horse's eye when being lunged. The noseband must be fastened firmly to prevent the cavesson from rubbing the horse's nose.

The cavesson can be fitted a little lower on the nose if the horse is not wearing a bridle. As a guide have the cavesson one finger's width below the cheekbone if the horse is wearing a bridle, and two fingers' width below the cheekbone if the horse is not wearing a bridle. The cavesson should not be fitted too low as this could damage the

nasal bone.

The **Wells cavesson** (Photo 3.3) is designed to fit lower on the nose and is therefore more severe. It should be fitted with the front nosepiece coming 25mm (1 inch) above the line of the top of the lips of the horse's mouth, with the straps fastened below the bit like a dropped noseband.

## Holding the lunge rein

The lunge rein must be correctly and tidily collect- ed in your hand so that it will easily feed out when required. When gathering up the lunge rein start collecting it from the end farthest from the fasten- ing so that the loops will slip off in order and will not get into a knot.

Once the rein is attached to the cavesson and fitted on the horse, you must collect your rein from the fastening end then turn over the pile of loops in your hand so that the rein will pay out correctly as described (see Photo 3.4).

*3.4*
*The lunge rein must be able to feed out of your hand smoothly.*

Never be tempted to coil the lunge rein around your hand as this can lead to a nasty injury if the horse should pull away and your hand is caught in the rein.

## Lungeing technique

When you lunge a horse you expect him to move forward and around you in a circle approximately 15-20m in diameter, making a true circle and taking a light contact on the lunge rein. The whip is used to encourage forward movement. When lungeing on the left rein, the handler holds the lunge rein in the left hand with the excess in the right so that he can shorten or lengthen the rein as necessary; the whip is also held in the right hand. When lungeing on the right rein, the positions are reversed. The horse should travel round the lunger, controlled within the vee shape formed by the lunge rein and the whip (see Fig. 6).

To start the horse lungeing, the handler will have to position himself slightly behind the horse so that he can effectively drive him forward.

When the horse is established in the art of lungeing, the handler should be able to stand more or less on one spot, turning with the horse as the latter moves round the circle. The lunger can then make the circle smaller or larger just by shortening or lengthening the lunge rein.

The arm holding the lunge rein should be bent at the elbow and the fingers closed around the rein. The contact should be comfortable for you and the horse. The lunge rein should never be allowed to drop to the ground. If this happens (when the horse cuts in on the circle) the rein should be shortened immediately.

The whip is used to encourage the horse to go forward. The lunger should hold it so that it points towards the horse's hindquarters, and so that it follows the horse as it moves round the circle. If the horse is nervous of the whip and running on too fast then the lunger must point the whip further away from the horse's rear. If necessary he can turn the whip away from the horse altogether, holding it behind himself instead. The whip can also be pointed towards the horse's shoulder to encourage him to keep away from you and out on the circle.

## The voice, and transitions

The horse must be taught to obey the voice commands as mentioned earlier. I always use *'whoa-oh'* when asking for halt as this is a soothing command and one that I would use instinctively to

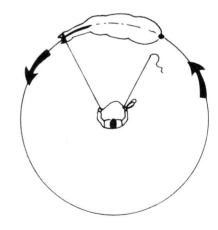

*Fig. 6  Lungeing on the left rein, showing the correct V-shape formed by lunge rein, handler and whip.*

calm a frightened horse. To ask for an upward transition into trot I say *'ter-rot'*, and for canter *'caaan-ter'*, raising the voice a little at the end of the command for an upward transition. For downward transitions I let the end of the word draw out and lower the voice as I do so, e.g. *'waa-alk'*, *'ter-rottt'*. The horse must have a clear idea of what is an upward and forward voice, and what is a downward and soothing voice.

## Starting to lunge

It is sometimes helpful, especially for the less-experienced lunger, to start a horse off with the aid of an assistant who can carry the whip, provided that he or she understands where to be and reacts correctly to the horse's actions.

I like to introduce the horse to the lungeing area by leading him on the right rein, in the manner

*3.5   Lead the horse round the area in which you are going to lunge him, so that he becomes familiar with his surroundings.*

*3.6   Lungeing on the left rein. The lunge rein in the left hand keeps a contact on the rein. The spare length of rein is coiled in the right hand ready to shorten and lengthen as necessary. The whip is held in the right hand to encourage the horse to move forward.*

*3.7   For a good contact on the cavesson, or if lungeing off the bit, the rein should be held as if you were riding the horse, i.e. with the lunge rein coming between the third and fourth fingers.*

*3.8   The lunge rein can be held in one hand, as shown here, when lungeing an experienced horse. However, if the horse is startled, the handler will be slower to collect up the contact on the rein and in doing so will move his whip more, which can further excite the horse.*

shown in Photo 3.5. I do this on the right rein for the following reason: if the horse is frightened or nervous of something outside the lunge area he will naturally move away from it and into the centre of the circle, which is empty. By positioning yourself between the horse and the source of his fear you can. gain his confidence and help him settle. You can stand in front of whatever has made him spook and talk to him, then gradually bring him to you and reassure him with a soothing stroke on the neck. Horses like to sniff objects and to investigate them, so let them satisfy their curiosity.

Having walked the horse round on the right rein several times, do the same on the left rein. You can then gently pay out the rein until the horse is moving on a circle of about 10m, on a long rein.

When lungeing on the left rein the whip is in your right hand and the lunge rein in the left hand with the surplus lunge rein in the right so that you can shorten and lengthen the rein as needed (see Photo 3.10). The lunge rein should always be taut but with a *light* contact. The feeling on the lunge rein is rather like the feeling on the reins when riding - it must be worked at until you have the correct feel which you and the horse can accept comfortably.

Some horses are happy to stay in walk on the lunge from the word go, but many take up trot

*3.12 - 3.14
When starting
a young horse
on the right
rein, first allow
him forward,
then out on a
larger circle.
The whip can
be used in the
right hand until
you can change
it over as shown
in Photos 3.15 -
3.17.*

3.9 - 3.11 *Starting a horse on the lunge with an assistant leading the horse on a circle. Gradually, the assistant lengthens the rein and takes the whip, or is dispensed with altogether.*

when they find themselves being driven away from their handler with little flicks of the whip. You must allow this and gradually teach the horse to adopt the pace you want through the use of your voice.

It may be necessary to drive the horse away from you in this way because he may feel a little lost and unsure of himself. Remember, he has never been taught to move away from his handler while being led and now you are asking him to take the initiative and move more on his own.

With the young horse, walk and trot are sufficient on the lunge to start with. Some naturally well-balanced horses will canter easily on the

lunge, but a lot of cantering on the lunge should be avoided until the horse is fit enough to stand the strain on his joints. 'All things in moderation' is the motto here, and common sense is essential. Anything which appears laboured or difficult for the horse should be avoided.

The whip is there purely to make the horse go forward, and if correctly used is simply another aid. It should not be an object of fear. The horse who is correctly started needs only a little flick with the whip to realise that he has to go away from it and therefore forward. As soon as he reacts in this way the whip should be held still but following, maintaining the V-shape shown in Fig. 6,

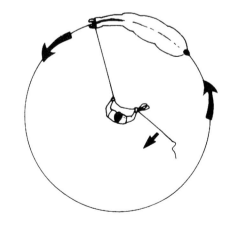

*Fig. 7   When the horse is nervous or moving too fast, take the whip further away until he settles.*

*3.15 - 3.17*
*Changing the whip from under the right arm to the left hand. Take the left hand behind your back and collect the whip with finger and thumb. Bring it behind your back and turn it round in your hand until it is in the normal driving position.*

with the whip pointing towards the horse's quarters, the lunge rein pointing towards his nose and yourself at the centre of the V. If the horse is moving forward too freely then the whip should drop back behind this V until the speed or pace is as required. The horse is steadied by your soothing, quiet voice.

There are various ways of slowing down a horse when first starting to lunge him but the main aim is for him to go forward. He should therefore be encouraged to do this by using the whip, so don't confuse him by then immediately trying to slow

him. Allow him to go forward at whatever pace he chooses and talk to him. He will slow down as he gains confidence in what you are doing.

When I do want to slow down or stop a horse on the lunge I prefer to use my voice coupled with a little vibration on the rein, then I release the rein saying 'Wa-alk' or 'Whoa-oh' until he responds. Also, positioning yourself so that you are slightly in front of the horse on the circle can help. Then, when you wish to send the horse forward again, move yourself back so that you are once more in a driving position. Remember to say 'Good boy' in a

soothing way as soon as the horse does as he is asked.

Too much chatter when lungeing a horse is a bad thing and any lack of concentration on your part can easily cause a bad habit. Problems can arise if you have not been observant enough to notice what the horse has been doing, or if you have neither rewarded the horse with a *'Good boy'* nor corrected him when he has dropped behind you and turned in to look at you. Training any animal requires your full concentration and, if given, the pupil will gain great respect for you.

## To make a true circle

Many horses fall in on one half of the circle and then pull away on the other half when being lunged. This is not satisfactory and must be overcome early on. Usually a horse will pull away in the general direction of the gate or door, or to wherever there is most space. If this happens the handler must correct the horse from pulling away with a firm hold on the lunge rein and a gentle release as soon as the horse responds and comes round on the circle. You must take care here that the horse does not get away from you; he must be taught to stay on the circle at all times.

To correct a horse who cuts in on the circle you have to be quick to shorten the lunge rein and move a little towards the forehand of the horse in an attacking manner. Look the horse in the eye and walk towards him in a stern and upright way, pointing the lunge whip at his shoulder. The horse will probably hasten to move away from you and may then pull out on the second half of the circle.

In bad cases it is a help to have an assistant with a lunge whip standing on the outside of the circle. This person can help to prevent the horse pulling away by waving the whip towards the horse to encourage it to move back onto the correct line. When it does so the handler can reward the horse with a more responsive feel on the lunge rein.

*3.18 - 3.20*
*The horse has been asked to 'whoa'. Place the whip away from the horse, under your right arm, and shorten the lunge rein as you approach the horse to reward him.*

If a horse has ever succeeded in getting away from its handler on the lunge, you must take extra care to prevent this happening again. Such a horse is likely to be very quick to try and get his own way again - so forewarned is fore-armed. Ideally you could enclose your lungeing ring with jump stands and rails; if this is not possible, lunge in the corner of a field, with an assistant standing in the open area away from the corner. If you have one, lunge the horse in a Wells cavesson, plus his bridle. If the horse lunges correctly with the lunge rein attached to the centre ring of the cavesson, then all is well, but if he tries to pull away or to turn away you will have to resort to lungeing off a check rein attached to the bridle as shown in Photo 5.3, p.51. If you lunge with this rein you must be sure to have a very responsive feel on the rein. This method should only be used as a corrective or emergency measure and you should return to using a cavesson as soon as is practicable.

## The paces on the lunge

The paces should be forward and balanced at all times.

♦ In the **walk** the horse should be encouraged to walk forward, showing a good overtrack (this is when the hind foot steps over the print of the fore foot). The horse should be allowed to use his head and neck.

♦ In the **trot** the horse should show lively impulsion, moving forward in the trot pace so that the hind foot is seen to be tracking up to the print of the fore foot. The trot should not appear hurried or running but should show rhythm and balance in the pace.

♦ The **canter** should be balanced and not too fast. Some horses find it difficult to balance in canter and should only be asked to canter for short periods until they improve their balance through the transitions of trot and canter. If the horse canters on the incorrect leg he must be brought back to trot before being asked again for the canter strike-off. Often young horses canter one half of the circle correctly and then change one

hind leg, becoming disunited. If this happens the horse must be brought back to trot before being asked to canter again.

## Problems on the lunge

Lungeing may appear a very straightforward activity but horses can react in many ways and they don't all walk and trot quietly in a perfect circle as we would like. As already mentioned, many cut in on the circle and then pull out on the opposite side. In this case you should move towards the horse in a more attacking manner and not retreat to collect up the rein which has become slack as he has moved in on the circle. You must point the whip at his shoulder and move towards him - almost placing yourself a little in front of him. You should look him firmly in the eye so he knows you are confronting him. Then stand firm when he tries to pull out on the opposite side of the circle and gently give him a few sharp jerks on the cavesson to make him listen to your voice. After a few rounds like this he will settle down and continue on the circle correctly.

**Turning in** - This is when a horse turns in to face the handler. When inexperienced lungers try to insist on a horse walking when he is first put on the lunge, they often come across this problem. They send him out on the lunge, he trots, they pull on the lunge rein to steady him and he turns in to look at them, wondering what he is to do. If you find yourself in this situation you have to decide whether the horse is being cheeky or is genuinely confused. If the latter, keep a fairly firm feel on the lunge rein, walk up to him, turn him into the correct direction and start him off again. If he continues to turn in, ask an assistant to correct him with a sharp flick with the whip on his upper hind leg while you keep the contact on the lunge rein. Be prepared to move slightly to the inside of the horse as he is driven forward. If you are lungeing singlehandedly you must 'attack' him with an aggressive stance, looking him firmly in the eye and chasing him back out onto the circle again. He must understand that the turning-in behaviour is not acceptable; and if you use a soothing voice when he is good and are careful to keep yourself in a driving position, he will learn to please you.

**Turning away** - There are a few horses who try to turn away from you when on the lunge. This can be very dangerous and usually only happens when the horse has been started incorrectly and has got away with this kind of behaviour before, either on the lunge or when being led. As I have said before, a horse never forgets and will try to repeat any ruse that has been successful - and, of course, these horses are always more difficult to change.

If a horse has got into the bad habit of turning away from you, you will have to resort to lungeing off the bit, via a check rein, to give you more control. In this case, the lunge rein should be threaded through the ring of the snaffle, passed over the head and attached to the bit ring on the other side (see Photo 5.3, p. 51). This works like a one-sided gag and does not pull across the jaw, which often makes horses lean out on the rein and is not to be recommended.

When lungeing a horse off the bit you must be more careful how you handle the lunge rein and be sure to have a light feel on the rein. If the horse suddenly tries to pull away from you, you must be quick and firm to stop him and turn him back, and then continue lungeing him. Remember that he will try to repeat the performance several times, so don't get caught out. A horse usually does the same thing at the same place on the circle, so anticipate his moves and make sure that you are one step ahead of his thinking. After all, it is our superior intelligence which helps us train and ride horses. Horses are simple, biddable creatures by nature; most love to please you and to be your friend.

## Duration and frequency of lungeing sessions

Because horses are individuals and all respond differently, some take longer to teach to lunge than others. Usually you will be able to train the horse to walk and trot on the lunge on the first day, and in both directions, but if the horse doesn't take to lungeing straightaway then only ask him to lunge on one rein during a session.

The horse should not be lunged until he is tired or distressed in any way. The maxim 'little and often' is what is needed for young horses. A lungeing session of approximately fifteen to twenty minutes is quite sufficient for a young horse. If the horse is not able to have any other form of exercise, such as a spell in the field, then it would be better for the horse to be worked twice a day on the lunge for twenty minutes. When the horse is fitter then thirty minutes is usually plenty of time in which to work it.

## Lungeing with a bit

Having taught your horse to lunge freely on both reins with a cavesson, over a few days you can introduce a snaffle bit and let him get used to the feel of it and learn to hold it correctly in his mouth. (The bit you choose may have to depend a little on trial and error - see Chapter 2.) The bit must be fitted correctly in the horse's mouth and should not be too low. The tongue must be under the bit and the horse should look comfortable with it.

Horses who are used to being bitted can go straight into a jointed snaffle. As already mentioned, I prefer a lightweight loose-ring jointed snaffle for my young horses and lunge them in it for a few days before introducing a roller.

I do this so that the horse can get used to the feel of the bit in his mouth without any pressure. He must enjoy having a bit in his mouth and great care must be taken when placing the bit in his mouth. Many horses have been spoilt through careless handling when bitting.

First, teach the horse to open his mouth: this is done by placing the left hand over the bridge of his nose, and slipping your fingers of your right hand into the side of his mouth (where he has no teeth!), pushing the tips of the fingers gently towards the roof of his mouth. The horse's natural reaction to this is to open his mouth. Often, people make the mistake of pulling down on the bars of the mouth, which only makes the horse resist and put his head up and it doesn't open the mouth wide.

When you have gently played with the horse's mouth in this way you can introduce the bit. Have the bit cradled over your thumb while your fingers are opening his mouth, then slip the bit into his mouth and place the bridle over his head. Some people find it easier to put the bridle on by holding the cheek pieces in the right hand (which has been passed under the horse's head and then placed over the bridge of the nose), letting the bit hang down between the lips and then opening the horse's mouth with the left hand.

Once the bridle is on, adjust the cheek pieces so that the bit is lying comfortably in the horse's mouth. The bit should lie so that there is just one slight wrinkle in the corner of the horse's lip.

Young horses can easily get inflamed lampas. This affects the roof of the mouth just behind the upper incisors. A young horse has very short teeth and if a bit is pulled out of the mouth when removing the bridle, the roof of the mouth can be bruised. Great care should be taken to open the horse's mouth when taking the bit out - in fact, just as much as when you put it in. This early correct

handling of the horse is so very vital.

If a horse has a dry mouth, it means that his tongue is very still and his jaw will be tense. This can be overcome by placing a little honey on the bit before you introduce it into his mouth, or you could try using a key bit for a few days.

## Putting on a roller

A roller is put on the horse to introduce him to the feel of a girth on a saddle, which he will meet later on.

I prefer to use a webbing roller for the first time as there is a bit more give in the feel of it. A leather roller with a webbing girth is equally suitable; and a girth with an elastic insert can be useful for very sensitive horses.

When first putting a roller on a young horse remember that he may react quite violently, so be prepared. If you have an assistant *always* place yourselves on the same side of the horse so that if the horse does react strongly he is controlled on one side and cannot kick anyone.

It is safer to introduce the roller to the horse in your lungeing area, rather than in the confines of a

*3.21 - 3.22   Placing a roller on a young horse for the first time. First allow him to sniff the numnah and/or*

*wither pad, and put these on and off his back several times, quietly and in a relaxed manner.*

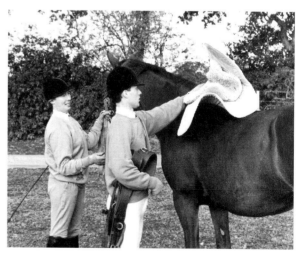

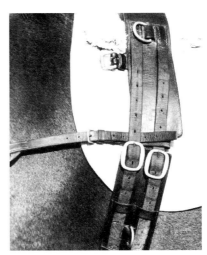

*3.24
The breast-girth strap is attached to the back strap of the roller and passes under the front one. This keeps it in place and prevents it slipping down the roller.*

*3.23    The roller. Always use a breastgirth to stop the roller slipping back, and a wither pad to prevent pinching the spine. A girth sleeve can prevent possible girth galls. A webbing or elastic insert in the girth allows the horse to breathe more easily.*

stable. The roller should always have a breastgirth attached to prevent it from slipping back. The girth should be made of soft material if possible, or encased in a sheepskin sleeve as young horses can easily develop girth galls as they are soft and fat at this stage in their lives. A wither pad or numnah will help to prevent pinching on the spine.

It is a good idea to let the horse smell the numnah or wither pad before placing it on his back. If he is nervous rub him on the shoulder and back before placing it in the correct position.

When placing the roller on the horse's back for the first time, lift it gently on and off his back a few times so he becomes accustomed to the feel of it before you place it on his back and let it sit there for a while. Attach the breast strap first and then, stroking the horse's girth area collect the other end of the roller and gently do it up, quite loosely to start with. I like to use an elastic girth or soft lampwick one.

*3.25 - 3.26    This horse has decided that she does not like the roller. Do not panic. Just keep the horse going*

*forward and talk to her soothingly. She will soon discover that nothing is hurting her and will accept the roller.*

The horse may object to the roller by bucking violently to start with, and this is quite natural. The main thing is to let him buck and when he finds that the roller doesn't hurt him, he will give up and quietly get on with the lungeing he has learned previously. Once he accepts the contact round his ribs you can gradually tighten up the roller. Lunge him on both reins and treat him normally.

## Introducing side-reins

When you have lunged the horse with a roller for a few days you can introduce side-reins. Side-reins are used to give the horse the feel of the reins to guide and balance him. Side-reins are either made of plain leather or nylon, and some have a rubber or elastic insert allowing for a 'giving' contact, which I prefer. However, the plainer type have their place for horses who lean on the rein and for training older horses.

When introducing side-reins it is essential that they are fitted loosely until the horse is trained to accept them. To start, adjust the side-reins so that when the horse is standing they will have hardly any contact.

The side-reins should be threaded through the girth straps to stop them slipping down. The end is

3.28 Detail showing side-rein clipped directly onto the bit. Make sure you attach the clip away from the horse. Note the already wet mouth.

passed under the roller, towards the horse's rear, brought back over the second girth strap and threaded under the first strap. If you have a roller with rings at the appropriate place then thread the side-rein under the roller, as above, and slip it through the ring to keep the side-rein in place. When you have adjusted the side-reins first clip the outside rein onto the cavesson (or bit) and then attach the inside one. The horse is now ready to be lunged.

Attach the side-reins to the side of the cavesson noseband until the horse is happy being lunged like this, then fasten them onto the bit and carry on lungeing as normal. Some horses dislike the side-

3.27 Loose side-reins attached directly to the bit.

3.29 Pull both side-reins towards you to check that they are the same length. The reins shown have an elastic insert.

3.30
*Starting the horse forward on the lunge with loose side-reins. Notice how the lunge rein passes between the third and fourth fingers with a light contact.*

reins attached to the noseband and show this by twisting the head about. If this happens place the side-reins directly onto the bit as shown in Photo 3.27.

The side-reins can be shortened gradually as the horse comes to accept their presence. This can be judged by observing the contact being taken on the outside rein and seeing if the horse relaxes his jaw and doesn't resist the side-reins by putting his head up and looking uncomfortable. The handler must take great care not to shorten the side-reins

too quickly as this can cause the horse to fight them; he could even rear up and hurt himself.

The horse should not be walked for too long in shortened side-reins as this can disturb the pace. In the early training the side-reins should be quite long so that they have little effect on the pace and help only to balance the horse.

All side-reins of any sort should be used with forward movement. Horses should not be put into short side-reins and asked to stand with their neck muscles taut for long periods. This is an ignorant

3.31  *Horse with no contact on the side-rein.*

3.32  *Horse accepting a light contact on the outside side-rein.*

and cruel practice. It also defeats the object of what you are trying to achieve, as when the horse is released from the reins his muscles will be so tired he will naturally want to relieve them by flexing in the opposite way, i.e. by putting his head up and throwing it about to relieve the tension that has been created. If the horse has been correctly lunged in side-reins, when they are released he will want to relax himself by lowering and stretching his neck.

## Saddling for the first time

When the horse is working confidently and correctly with the side-reins attached to the roller, you can teach him to carry a saddle on his back. I like to let the horse sniff the saddle before putting it on him, tactfully introducing it in the same way as the roller - gently on and off - until the horse is not nervous of the saddle, before doing up the girth. To begin with I would recommend that you use an old saddle, not your best one, and remove the stirrup irons and leathers.

Initially I always put on a breastplate, so that the girth need not be done up too tightly, which could

*3.33 Horse being lunged with saddle and side-reins attached. The horse is accepting both a light contact on the side-reins and the bit, walking in a correct outline.*

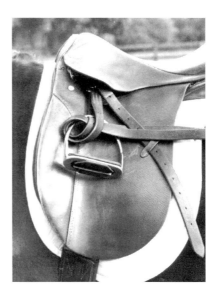

*3.34 Saddle with stirrups attached and secured for lungeing a young horse. Later, the irons can be let down and allowed to flap, but they must be short enough not to get anywhere near the horse's elbow.*

startle the horse. Allow the horse time to accept the different weight of the saddle on his back.

When the horse appears settled, fasten up the breastplate and gently do up the girth. Lead the horse forward in the normal manner and gradually start to lunge him on the left rein. If he bucks because he dislikes the saddle, just let him get used to it, talking to him and reassuring him until he accepts the strange object on his back. Once he has settled, lunge him in the usual way on both reins and adjust the girth as necessary. The horse will already be familiar with the feeling of wearing something around his middle through having worn a roller, so you should be able to fasten the girth a little tighter than you did initially with the roller.

It is very important that you avoid frightening the horse by allowing the saddle to be so loose that it can slip round his belly and get underneath him. This can easily happen and the horse can become very upset. Make sure, then, that you are able to do up the girth tightly enough to prevent the saddle slipping. Of course, using a breastplate with the girth will help to keep the saddle in a good position.

After a few days, when the horse has accepted the saddle, it is a good idea to attach stirrup leathers and stirrup irons, so that the horse gets used to them flapping along his sides. The leathers must be short enough to prevent the stirrups from banging against the horse's elbows, which could be quite painful. Adjust the leathers so that the stirrups hang just at the bottom edge of the saddle flap, and no lower. The horse can be lunged with the stirrups hanging down. He may not like the irons flapping about on his sides but they usually cause little trouble.

Once the horse is used to the saddle and the stirrup irons you can lunge him with the side-reins attached to the girth. These should be fastened beneath the saddle flap, just about level with the bottom of the flap. To prevent them from slipping down the girth, attach the side-reins as for lungeing in a roller.

Over several days the horse will learn to accept the side-reins and saddle and start to carry himself in a balanced way with an arched neck, seeking the gentle support of the side-rein. This will help him to use his neck and back muscles correctly, thus strengthening them before you start to ride him.

I feel strongly that this early training must not be rushed if you wish to have a horse with a good mouth and correct balance when you come to ride him. As you gradually shorten the side-reins and lunge the horse forward, so the horse takes up the contact on the outside rein. This is regulated by the feel on the lunge rein and the forward driving from the whip. This is the essence of the feel you will have when riding the horse and it is at this time that you start to teach the horse about this two-way communication.

## Cantering on the lunge

When the horse is well balanced he can be taught to canter on the lunge. This must only be done on good going and the horse should be asked to canter just one or two circles before making a transition back to trot again. He can be allowed to canter in side-reins but only if he is happy with them and is already working in a balanced way in walk and trot.

Cantering young horses on the lunge does depend on the balance of each individual horse. If

*3.35   When the young horse is well balanced he can be asked to canter on the lunge.*

the horse is not balanced then he should not be chased round in an unbalanced way. It is better to teach him to be in balance in walk and trot and to progress to canter later.

Older horses can be cantered on the lunge for longer periods as they are strong and mature in their physique.

## Transitions on the lunge

Teaching the horse to go from one pace to another and back again will help with the acceptance of the rein, but the handler must be sure that the horse goes from trot to walk correctly, walking forward into the rein and then forward into trot again.

When the forward transitions are understood then the horse must be taught to halt in the side-reins and to walk on (and later trot) out of halt. This is a good exercise and helps to strengthen the back muscles.

Transitions from walk to trot, trot to canter, canter to trot and trot to walk can all be practised on the lunge when the horse is relaxed and working in a nice, balanced outline in the side-reins. If he has progressed successfully to this stage then he is ready for the introduction of a second lunge rein, i.e. for long-reining.

## Martingales and training aids

I very rarely find it necessary to use any training aids but some can be usefully employed with certain horses at different stages of their training.

♦ The **standing martingale** - this is the simplest training aid. It consists of an adjustable strap which is attached to the girth between the horse's front legs, passes through a neck strap and is attached to a cavesson noseband. This device prevents the horse from throwing his head up when evading the bit and thereby possibly hitting the rider in the face. It is sometimes a useful precaution when first backing a young horse - the neck strap is certainly a handy aid for the rider.

♦ **Running martingale** - this is attached to the girth in the same way as the standing martingale but divides into two branches at the neck strap, each branch ending in a ring through which the reins are passed. The running martingale acts on the bars of the mouth and comes into action when the head is raised. I would not use this device when lungeing.

♦ **Draw reins** - these are long reins which can be fitted in many ways for both lungeing and riding. If used correctly they can be a useful training aid; some people use them instead of side-reins and some favour them for certain horses. I find them useful for horses who are weak in the back.

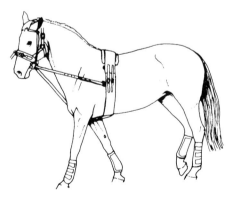

Fig. 8    Draw reins come into action when the horse's head is raised.

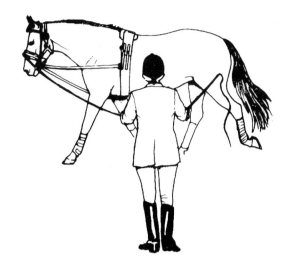

Fig. 9    Lungeing in draw reins.

My preferred way of fitting them for lungeing is to take them from the girth, pass them between the front legs, through the rings of the snaffle bit then back to the roller, where they are attached at about halfway up the ribcage. They must be fitted very loosely to start with and shortened only gradually. With this rein the horse can stretch his neck forward thus helping his back muscles to come up and the hind legs to work more under the body.

I don't like the method of using draw reins where they are fitted to the girth straps at the side of the horse and then run up to the rider's hand via the bit as this concertinas the horse's weight onto the hand and pulls the head in towards the chest. This causes the horse to get very strong in the hand and eventually to bolt.

If draw reins are fitted for riding I prefer to take them from the girth, between the horse's front legs, pass them through the bit rings and up to the rider's hand. When employed correctly the draw reins only come into action when the horse's head is too high and they release automatically when the horse's head is in the right position.

♦ The **Market Harborough** or **German rein** - this is a type of draw rein which is attached to the

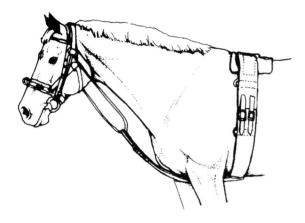

Fig. 10   The Chambon.

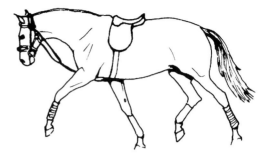

Fig. 11   The Chambon in action.

normal reins of the bridle. When correctly adjusted it only comes into operation when the horse's head carriage is too high and releases when the horse's outline is correct (much like my preferred draw-rein fitting described above).

♦ The **Chambon** - this is a rein which can be helpful in teaching the horse to lower his head and use his back. It is useful for a very green horse with no natural muscle on his back and for a horse with a ewe-neck.

The Chambon consists of a headstrap with a ring at either end; this fits onto the headpiece of the bridle. A nylon cord with a clip at each end is attached to the bit rings, runs up through the headstrap rings and is attached in front of the chest to an elasticated side-rein which passes between the forelegs and is secured to the girth.

When the horse raises his head the bit is taken upwards in the mouth and pressure will be felt on the nerve centre at the poll. The horse has the freedom to lower his head and move it from side to side. Obviously this device must be fitted loosely and gradually tightened (via the central side-rein) one hole at a time as the horse becomes confident.

The Chambon has the advantage that it doesn't put any pressure on the bars of the mouth, and I feel it is possibly safer (and kinder) to use than side-reins if they are mis-used. I feel that the Chambon has a good effect on the back and hind legs of the horse, and correct lungeing with this device can help the horse's physique.

♦ The **De Gogue** - this is a device for ridden work, but perhaps deserves a mention here. It is a variation of the Chambon, the difference being that the nylon cord passes through the bit ring and runs back to the central strap. It can therefore put pressure on the bars of the mouth. When correctly adjusted it automatically releases its effect when the horse lowers its head and neck.

# 4. Long-Reining the Young Horse

Long-reining is used to help teach the horse the leg and rein aids, to accustom the horse to objects around his hind legs, and to help balance the horse through the increased activity of the hind legs.

## Equipment

♦ Saddle with stirrups and leathers.
♦ Snaffle bridle.
♦ Three-ring lungeing cavesson with two lunge reins 7.2m (24 feet) long.
♦ Stirrup strap (a strap or length of twine which is attached to both stirrups to stop them moving about when the lunge reins are threaded through the stirrups).
♦ Four brushing boots.

♦ An assistant with a lunge whip.

## Introducing the long reins

When introducing a horse to long reins or to a second lunge rein you must take care how you hold the reins. It is very easy to get into trouble as you now have a lot of rein to control.

I like to have an assistant (who should wear gloves) to hold the horse while I acquaint the horse with the feel of the lunge rein on his hind legs. The assistant stands on the near side and holds the horse with one lunge rein attached to the near-side ring of the cavesson. The other rein is attached to the offside cavesson ring (Photo 4.2), passed through the stirrup iron on that side, then taken at

4.1
The stirrup irons are secured by a strap which passes under the horse's belly.

4.2
Long-reins attached to the cavesson.

*4.3 The handler moves at a safe distance, while the assistant remains at the horse's head.*

*4.4 The handler moves the lunge rein very gently so that it touches the horse's side.*

a safe distance from the horse to the rear (Photos 4.3-4.4).

The handler moves the lunge rein very gently so that it touches the horse's side and offside hind leg. If the horse objects, by kicking or appearing nervous, ease off the contact completely until the assistant reassures him that nothing will harm him, then gently walk round with the rein again until it touches his side and hind leg and he is happy to accept this contact. This could take some time and you may only progress to this stage on the first day.

**Please remember that all horses can kick. Never take a stupid risk; always be at a safe distance, especially with a young horse.**

## Starting work with two reins

Having acquainted the horse with the feel of the second rein on his offside hind leg, you can start to lunge him on the left rein in walk, but with the second rein lying over the saddle (Photo 4.5). The stirrup irons, resting just below the saddle flap, should be secured by a strap (shown in Photo 4.1) which passes under the horse's belly, linking one iron to the other.

When the horse is settled in walk allow the second rein to drop over his croup (Photo 4.6) and then down behind him. If he is startled by this, on

no account pull on the rein; just keep the rein well off the ground and carry on lungeing as usual, talking to the horse in a soothing voice. Gradually he will settle and you can then take a little more pressure on the outside rein. This activates the hind legs and makes the horse bring them more under his body, thus supporting the horse's weight in a better way and preparing him for more collection.

Having worked the horse on the left rein in walk and trot, change the rein and repeat the exercise on the right rein.

*4.5 Starting to lunge the horse in walk.*

4.6   *Allowing the rein to drop over the horse's croup.*

4.9   *All horses can kick, so take care!*

4.7   *Keep the rein loose but off the ground. The horse looks apprehensive.*

4.10   *This horse is showing signs of temper. He dislikes the pressure on the cavesson.*

4.8   *If the horse resists, do not pull on the rein; just use a soothing voice.*

4.11   *When the horse settles, you can apply a little more pressure on the outside rein.*

## Changing the rein

To change the rein you must bring the horse to a halt and ask your assistant to hold him while you reorganise the lunge reins for the other direction. When you start to move towards the horse, shorten up your reins as you approach. Begin by taking up the left rein, one loop at a time, then the right, alternately, so that you arrive beside the horse with both reins correctly coiled in your hands. Give the left rein to your assistant while you walk, at a safe distance, behind the horse and come up on his off-side, lengthening and collecting up the reins as you go. Pass the rein through the stirrup iron and adjust the horse's position for long-reining on the right rein.

When gathering up your reins you could flick the right rein over the horse's back, but I would not recommend that you do this in the early stages as it could easily frighten the horse. However, once the horse is more experienced you should be able to do this without upsetting him. Photos 4.15-4.20 show the method I use.

Only when the horse is entirely happy and relaxed about the long reins touching his hind legs and on both reins, can you progress to working the

4.12
The long reins attached to the bit.

horse with the long reins attached to the bit (see Photo 4.12). If you are using a roller and not a saddle with stirrup irons you must be sure that your long reins will run freely through the roller's D-rings. If they snag they will prevent a good contact on the bit or cause the bit to be pulled to one side as they don't release quickly enough.

4.13 - 4.14   When the horse is happily accepting the long reins attached to the bit and running through the outside stirrup, you can progress to working with the reins running through both stirrups, as shown on p. 45.

*4.15 - 4.20    Shortening up double reins on an experienced horse.*

## Lungeing from behind and introducing turns

When you are satisfied that the horse is working well on the long reins with one rein running through the stirrup on the offside (Photo 4.13-4.14), you can start to drive the horse around with the inside rein through the stirrup iron as well. First, lunge him on a circle so that he becomes used to this form of exercise, and when you and he are ready you can start to teach him to turn and go the other way. This is done by bringing him back to walk, turning him by taking a little more pressure on the outside rein and then allowing him to turn away, so putting him onto the other rein. This should be a gradual process whereby the horse learns to turn away from you, out of the circle and onto a new circle. Always remember to keep the circle as large as possible, especially with a young horse.

If the horse is relaxed and happy about walking in the long reins and changing the rein in this way,

you can start introducing trot transitions. Try the following exercise: trot on the right rein, come back to walk, trot again, bring him back to walk and change the rein, using a little pressure on the outside rein. It is important to talk to the horse while asking for transitions from one pace to another.

## Driving the horse forward

Provided the horse is confident thus far and is not bothered by seeing you sometimes behind him, you could try driving him in walk around a small field or your school. He has to learn that the reins are there to drive him forward as well to guide him.

When walking behind the horse make sure that you are at least 2m (6ft) away from his hind legs.

To move him forward you have to use the rein with a slight flapping movement near the stirrup area, while you ask with the voice saying 'Walk on'. Teach the horse to 'whoa' or halt by applying a little pressure on the reins and saying 'Whoa-oh', so that soon the horse learns to stop and then walk on again with a little flapping from the rein and some encouragement from your voice.

*4.21 - 4.22    First, drive the horse around the arena...*

*...and when nearly behind him, make a small turn.*

*4.23- 4.24   Making a small half circle in walk to the left. When settled, move more behind the horse and*   *attempt a half circle to the right.*

## Coping with problems

Long-reining is fine as long as everything is going smoothly, but sometimes horses become frightened and when this happens you must be quickly in a position where you can turn the horse. If you are directly behind him when he panics you will never be able to stop him as he is far stronger than you are. In the early training, when you are driving him about and teaching him how to turn, try always to be just a little to one side of the horse so that he can see you and knows that you are there all the time.

At any sign of panic, the horse should be brought onto a circle and lunged so that you can reassure him. Bring him back to walk and allow him to relax before continuing with work on straight lines. In time he will take to it calmly and with confidence.

Long-reining teaches a horse to steer and it is also a very good way of teaching a young pony not to be frightened if a rider has the misfortune to fall off and be dragged with his foot in the stirrup. Long-reining gets the horse used to objects around his hind legs and he is then far less likely to kick at a person on the ground.

Long-reining can be of great advantage to you provided that you have good hands and work the horse correctly. If the horse resists the long reins, it usually means that your hands are not light enough, in which case it is better to proceed by riding the horse and abandoning the long-reining altogether. Only you can judge this but you must be aware that the horse will object if the long reins are too heavy or if your hands are too heavy on his mouth. This may be apparent when the horse is asked to halt and walk on.

Downward transitions will also show you

*4.25   Shortening the reins for a left turn.*

4.26 - 4.30
(Clockwise, from bottom right)
*Turning to the right and going forward to trot on the circle.*

whether the horse is uncomfortable and dislikes the long reins. To remedy this you must make your handling much lighter and more acceptable to the horse. If the horse resists and backs off the rein, then you must drive him up to the reins lightly but still with a contact that is acceptable to him. Sometimes, if the horse is rather 'mouthy', this is easier to do when you are riding. You must carry your hands with a bent elbow - just as you would carry them when riding.

Some trainers like to keep side-reins on a horse when they are long-reining. This does mean that you have perhaps a little more control, but I would certainly let the side-reins out at least four or five holes. Side-reins can be a help in that they keep the horse a little more balanced and you don't have to do quite so much balancing from your own hands.

Long reins are difficult to control and the closer to the horse you become, the easier it is. But, of course, you must remember that a horse can kick, and if you are close to him you can easily get hurt. You must stay at a safe distance at all times until you can trust your horse completely. All teaching should be carried out at a safe distance.

## An alternative method of long-reining

Another way of using long reins is to take a second rein through the turrets of a driving roller and over the horse's back. This method is useful for making the horse more manoeuvrable and to help him accept the outside rein. You cannot drive the horse from behind in the conventional way, though, since the horse is effectively kept on the lunge and driven only from the roller.

Provided the horse is kept driven up to the reins in the normal manner, you can use this method to work him, to teach him to accept the bit, and to introduce him to being steered from the reins. It is especially useful for a horse who bears down on the reins and jerks his head forward. If you maintain a quiet contact on the rein as you lunge him and change direction he will come to accept the reins with grace.

Despite the above advantages I seldom use this method with my horses as I don't find it easy to progress the work with the long reins fitted in this way.

## Learning about the leg aids - through the long reins

The horse is now ready to have the weight of a rider put on his back and to start being ridden. If you don't have a suitable rider you can still work the horse gainfully from the ground, teaching him to move away from the rein and thus using the rein much as you would your leg. You must be prepared, though, to take your time and to use the reins quietly and firmly.

If you are walking behind the horse, say, around a field, you can start to teach the horse to move sideways a little, away from one rein (i.e. away from the leg). Do this by keeping one rein a little firmer and flapping the other rein gently against his side until he steps away from it. As soon as he responds correctly reward him with a well-earned 'Good boy' and cease flapping with the rein. Then flap the rein again until he walks away from it once more, praise him with your voice, and continue in this fashion. Do the same with the other rein so that he learns to step away from both reins.

Gradually he will come to understand that when you flap just one rein, he must move away from it, but if you flap both reins he must move straight forward. You must teach this exercise quietly and patiently, giving the horse time to understand the differences between the aids over a few days. In this way you will have taught him to answer the leg, both forwards and sideways, in readiness for a rider.

## Leg-yielding and shoulder-in

You can now progress to teaching the leg-yielding movement, in which the horse walks forward and sideways from the rein (Photo 4.31). When that is established you can move on to the shoulder-in

*4.31   Starting leg-yielding. This horse is a little resistant, and taking too much pressure on both reins. In a few more steps he will understand and move more evenly with sideways steps.*

*4.32   Introducing shoulder-in. The horse is nicely contained by the outside rein and showing a slight bend to the inside throughout his body.*

(Photo 4.32), pushing him with the right rein into the left rein (for right shoulder-in). Here you push his quarters into the outside long rein, which controls his quarters. The inside rein takes his shoulders in while the outside rein prevents the outside shoulder from falling outwards.

If you and your horse have mastered the techniques thus far, you may want to try working through some of the more advanced long-reining exercises described in Chapter 7.

## Finishing the long-reining session

Always take care how you collect up your reins at the end of a session. First of all, it is helpful to have an assistant at the horse's head, standing at the near side. You can then shorten the reins and come up beside the horse on the near side, shortening both reins as you approach. Always stay at a safe distance where, if the horse is startled, his kick cannot reach you. Don't come up too close behind the horse - make sure that you place yourself well to the side where he can see you.

As you near the horse, flick the outside rein over the horse's back so that it lies on the saddle or across his back. Place the shortened outside rein across the saddle. Continue shortening the reins until you are level with his shoulders. Thread the inside rein through the stirrup and pass it to the assistant. Go round the front of the horse, detach the outside rein from the cavesson or the bit, slip it through the stirrup iron and remove it.

# 5. Backing and Riding Young Horses

When backing and riding young horses it is most important not to hurt the horse in any way. Whilst backing should not be traumatic for the horse you should be aware that it involves new experiences and sensations and a change of perspective in the horse's mind. One minute you are on the ground, where he has learned to accept you as a friend and mentor, and the next you are sitting on his back giving him signals which feel strange to him. However, if you have been lungeing the horse and long-reining him, this will have prepared him reasonably well for seeing you behind him and then to one side, and part of the groundwork will have been done.

Backing a horse for the first time is usually very easy for the youngster who has been correctly handled, has a sensible respect for you and is obedient. However, it is much more difficult for the nervous horse or one who is naturally timid. Both types can be frightened and the latter more easily, so care and attention to detail are extremely important. For instance, don't mount and find that the girths are too loose, that your stirrup leathers are not the correct length, or that the tack is flimsy and could break. All these things can be avoided. If you do have to tighten the girth before mounting, walk the horse forward or lunge him for a few minutes before trying to mount him.

The rider should check that the stirrups are approximately the right length by placing his hand on the stirrup bar and extending the stirrup towards his armpit. If it just reaches the armpit it will be about the right length for riding. If the nearside stirrup leather is twisted just above the stirrup,

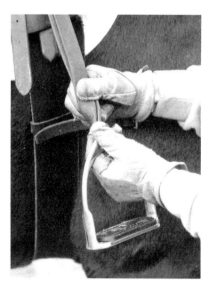

5.1
Twist the off-side stirrup leather so that it is correctly placed for the rider to place his foot.

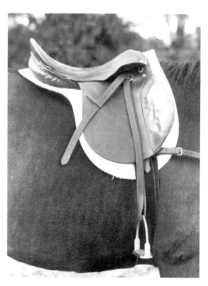

5.2
The stirrup leather twisted ready for the rider's right foot.

the stirrup will be correctly positioned for the rider to put his foot in when mounted. In this way he won't upset the horse by fiddling to find the stirrup. (See Photos 5.1-5.2.)

Before you begin the mounting session make sure that you have the following:

♦ An experienced rider.
♦ An experienced assistant.
♦ Breastgirth or breastplate.
♦ Saddle strap or neck strap.

The person who has initially taught the horse to lunge, provided that he is competent, should be on the ground and in charge of lungeing the horse with a rider, as the horse will have confidence in this handler. However, if the horse is not trusting and obedient on the lunge then a more capable trainer should take over for a few days prior to mounting. This should give him time to make the horse listen, by asking for a lot of transitions from

*5.3   In preparation for being mounted for the first time, the horse is fitted with a check rein.*

walk and halt, until the horse is obedient.

I know many people who first mount their horses inside a stable, and have done so all their lives, but I do not recommend this practice and consider it extremely dangerous, especially if the horse panics. For the same reason, I personally would never introduce a horse to a roller or saddle in a stable, but always do it outside in the lungeing area where there is plenty of room for manoeuvre.

However, there are times when circumstances do not allow you to proceed as you wish, especially if you have to cope single-handed. So if you *do* have to put a roller on a horse for the first time in a stable, be aware that the horse could react violently. Make sure that you are in a position to make a quick exit and cannot get trapped against the wall by a horse going crazy in a confined space. And do make sure that the stable is safe for the horse by removing any buckets, haynets etc. beforehand. I mention this only to make people realise how easy is to have stupid accidents; with a little care and forethought many of these could be avoided. What we want to end up with is a happy horse and a confident rider, not a pair of gibbering wrecks!

## The first mounting session

The day you attempt to mount the horse for the first time is usually two, or at the most three, weeks after you have started him on the lunge. By this time he should be confident about being saddled up.

A breastplate or breastgirth should be fitted to help keep the saddle in place and to stop the girth slipping back. The breastplate is usually made of leather. It is fitted over the horse's neck as follows: the strap with an adjustment is passed between the front legs of the horse and threaded through the girth straps; and the two short straps are attached to the lower dees on the saddle. If fitted correctly you should be able to place your fist between the neck and the strap and it not be tight.

The breastgirth is normally made of webbing and leather and is adjusted so that a fist can be fitted comfortably between the shoulder and the webbing strap. Take care to see that the webbing is not pulling on the point of shoulder; it should be between the base of the neck and the shoulder (see Photo 3.23, p.33).

A saddle strap can be fitted to the saddle to provide a useful hand-hold for the rider if the horse reacts violently. It comprises a piece of rolled leather fitted over the pommel, running between the upper dees of the saddle. Alternatively, a simple neck strap - either a stirrup leather or a neck strap from a martingale - will do the same job. It is placed over the base of the neck for the rider to hold for support if needed.

The horse will need lungeing on both reins and should be kept working well forward so that he works off any excess energy. When he has settled bring him to a halt and check the girth and leathers.

Before mounting I always put a check rein on the horse (see Photo 5.3), because if he panics it is not possible to control him in a cavesson. The horse is now ready for mounting practice.

The rider and assistant must *not* be novices. They must both be familiar with the 'leg up' method of mounting. (A 'leg up' is when an assistant hold the rider's left leg at the knee and ankle, so that the rider can spring lightly into the saddle without placing his left foot in the stirrup to mount.) By mounting in this way the saddle is not disturbed, there is less danger of the rider losing his balance if the horse should move, and there is no likelihood of the rider's left toe prodding the horse's side, as could easily happen when mounting from the stirrup.

After the initial period of lungeing take the horse into the centre of your lungeing circle, ready for mounting. The rider should double-check the stirrups then quietly place his hand on the centre of the saddle. While he does this the lunger should stay on the near side, talking to the horse to reassure him. The rider, standing on the near side, is quietly given a 'leg up' by the assistant so that the rider finishes up leaning across the saddle (Photo 5.4). This can be repeated several times until the horse is quite calm and confident about the movement made by the rider.

Now the rider can be given a 'leg up' and stay in a more upright position, as shown in Photo 5.5. The horse will be able to see him much as he will when he has a rider actually sitting in the saddle on his back. Repeat this exercise several times; the more the horse becomes accustomed to the rider's presence up there, the better. Sometimes, I find it a good thing to move the horse a few steps and then

*5.4   The rider is given a 'leg up' and leans across the saddle...*

*5.5   ...later he will stay more upright so that the horse sees the rider higher up behind him.*

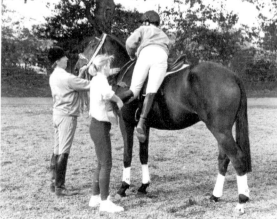

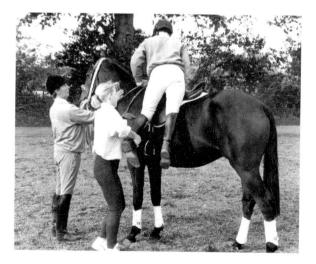

*5.6 - 5.7   Mounting the horse and placing the rider...*

*...gently into the saddle with a 'leg-up'.*

stop again while the rider remains in this position across his back. I would only do this if the horse looked happy and confident in his eye.

A horse who is tense, with his eyes looking back and ears moving back and forward, is not confident. If you see these signs just continue to mount and dismount lots of times, everyone staying calm and relaxed throughout. If the horse does tense up and move quickly forwards or side-ways, the handler should reassure him by holding him firmly and stroking him on the neck.

Take your time. If the horse is very nervous, lunge him for a few minutes then repeat the mounting exercise.

In some cases this will be enough for the horse to absorb in one day; in others you can proceed to mounting the horse fully (Photos 5.6-5.7).

Mount and dismount from the near side to begin with, and if the horse is relaxed, the lunger can move to the offside and allow the rider to dis-mount on that side too. Do this several times so that the horse becomes accustomed to movement on both sides.

It is important that the lunger stands on the dis-mounting side (until you can fully trust the horse) because if the horse were suddenly to be startled by the rider as he got off, the rider could possibly be knocked over by the horse or kicked. If, however, the lunger is on the same side as the dismounting rider he can control the horse and the horse's hind

legs will move away from the rider.

## First steps on the mounted horse

When rider and horse are confident about mounting and dismounting it is time to ask the horse to move with the rider on board. At first, the lunger should walk the horse forward for a few steps then stop and stroke him (Photo 5.8). Repeat this several times before progressing to leading him on a circle and asking him to walk on in a free walk (Photo 5.9).

The rider should sit quietly, just talking gently to the horse. This is all the rider should do for the first few days. The rider's legs should lie quietly against the horse's sides, and it is better for the rider to hold onto the saddle strap or neck strap than risk losing his balance if the horse should move un-expectedly. In this way the horse gains confidence in the burden on his back.

The lunger can gently ease the horse out (in walk) onto a longer lunge rein (see Photos 5.10-5.11), but only if the horse looks happy. If the horse tenses up, the lunger must stop the horse, go to him to reassure him, then lead him on again and gradually return to walking on the lunge.

Most horses accept all this quite easily and, if so, you can introduce some trot work. Just let the horse trot a few strides (see Photo 5.12) and then

5.8   *When the horse is reassured, you can proceed.*

5.9   *First lead the horse quietly on a circle. Here, an assistant carries a whip to encourage the horse to go forward, if necessary.*

ask him to walk again. To start, I find it better for the rider to stay in sitting trot until the horse looks confident and happy, is carrying his tail and his eyes look quiet. If the horse is nervous bring him back to walk and reassure him. It is sometimes helpful to encourage the rider to talk quietly all the time so that the horse gets used to hearing a voice from on top of him. When the horse is settled and happy ask him to trot again, and just go on in this way until he is confident in both walk and trot.

The rider must sit comfortably on the horse in an upright and very supple position, taking care not to get left behind the movement if the horse tenses up and moves quickly forward. The better balanced the rider, the easier it is for the horse. The rider should take a light feel on the reins to help the horse balance himself with the extra weight of the rider.

5.10 - 5.11   *Allow the horse out on a longer rein...*

*...as he gains confidence.*

5.12   *When the horse looks happy, you can attempt a trot.*

5.13   *After a few days, and when you can trust the horse, the lunge rein can be placed on the cavesson again. The horse is moving freely forward and accepting the contact from the rider's seat and leg aids.*

With some rather cheeky horses, once they have accepted the presence of the rider on their back, it is sometimes better to carry on quietly on day one until they are settled with the rider in walk and trot on both reins. No two horses are the same, but whatever happens, *never overwork a horse.* This will leave him with tired muscles and he is more likely to play up the next day if everything aches.

After all, riding the horse should be a pleasure for both parties, not a pain.

Over several days you will be able to progress to riding the horse off the lunge and making gradual changes of direction.

It is essential that the early riding of the horse is

5.14   *Here you see the horse off the lunge, happily accepting a light contact and obeying the rider.*

5.15   *Another three-year-old showing good paces and carrying himself in a good outline.*

not hurried. A trainer must be able to assess what the horse can cope with in one day. With most horses, it is better to do a little less than too much; and always try to avoid trouble. An unexpected distraction, such as a young child suddenly appearing or making a noise, could spell disaster; likewise a dog or cat rushing headlong into the lungeing area to greet you could also have the same effect. Think ahead, and plan for the smoothest start.

# 6. Lungeing Over Fences

Lungeing young horses over fences can be a very useful way of teaching them to jump, without the burden of the rider's weight. Correctly performed, the horse can gain a lot of experience in jumping and the owner can assess the horse's ability and attitude towards jumping.

Loose jumping is excellent too, but it requires a very experienced trainer and many more people and facilities if it is to be carried out effectively. Also, loose jumping can easily frighten or upset a horse unless it is very carefully organised. Therefore, before any loose jumping is attempted the temperament of the horse should be studied carefully.

Loose jumping can be very successfully employed with the lazy type of horse, who needs to go forward and open up over a jump, but the sharper, more highly strung horse can become very excited and rush over his fences, losing his natural jumping style.

I recently came across an ingenious method of inducing loose jumping naturally. It consisted of a number of small fences made of telegraph poles, set up on a well-turfed lane used by youngsters on their way in for feeding. This gave the owner an insight into the jumping potential of his young-stock and also the chance to see which ones were the bold, natural jumpers.

However, horses who have been loose-schooled can be difficult to keep in a field. Once you have trained them to jump loose they can just jump wherever they like - and one I knew even jumped back into his stable! On the other hand, horses who have been taught to jump on the lunge or under saddle don't necessarily exhibit this trait.

Lunged horses seem to have faith in the handler, and whilst they are happy to jump with the lunge rein attached, they appear lost and bewildered if suddenly asked to jump while loose, even if the fence is very small.

## The jumping area

When starting to jump your horse on the lunge, it is important to start with a safe arena. An indoor school, free of distractions, is ideal.

Good footing is essential if your horse is to have confidence in his jumping. If you are unable to use an indoor school, an outdoor manège is quite acceptable, or you could work in the corner of a field if the ground is suitable.

A deep, boggy or hard, slippery surface will quickly destroy a horse's natural jump. He will be unsure of his footing and will want to get his feet back on the ground as soon as possible. As a result he will learn to hit the poles and not care, for his attention will be focused on keeping his feet.

## Equipment

When lungeing for jumping the horse should wear protective boots on all four legs, and over-reach boots on both front pasterns. Knee-caps and a bridle are optional. A lungeing cavesson, whip and lunge rein will also be required.

For the fence materials you will need four to six poles, two jump wing stands and four 'Bloks' (plastic jump supports).

6.1   A horse correctly dressed for being lunged over fences.

6.2   Start by leading the horse over the poles, saying 'Walk on'. If you position yourself slightly in front of the horse, this will give him confidence.

## Introducing the horse to poles and jump wings

Begin by leading your horse around the arena, just as you did on the first day you started to lunge him. Show him some jump stands and a few poles on the ground. Then walk over the poles yourself, saying 'Walk on', and he will follow. Do this several times until he is relaxed and confident in what he is doing. Praise him and stroke him on the neck. The horse is now ready to be lunged over poles on the ground.

6.3   This horse is trotting over the poles exceptionally well for his first attempt. Most horses are not so neat and it takes them several attempts to find the correct rhythm.

6.4   On the second attempt the horse is showing activity with both knees and hocks, and a more casual air about his balance.

## Working over poles on the ground

The poles should be set out 1.3-1.35m (4ft 3ins-4ft 6ins) apart for the horse to trot over - the longer distances being for the bigger-striding horse. (Ponies will obviously need the poles a little closer together, depending on the size on the pony and the individual's stride length. As a guide, a 12.2hh pony will need the poles 15cms (6ins) closer; and a 14.2hh pony will want the distances shortened by 7.5cms (3ins).) Put down one to three poles depending on the attitude and temperament of the horse. With nervous horses, start with only one pole and build up gradually.

When you start lungeing the horse, lunge away from the poles and slowly work the horse nearer to them so that he does not become anxious about their presence (see Fig. 12, p.65). When you are happy with the horse's attitude move nearer the poles and say 'Trot on' as he approaches them. He may need a slight flick with the whip, but try to avoid this as you don't want to frighten him. If he trots over the poles, praise him with your voice. Continue lungeing him until he settles into a good trot rhythm - he will probably be unbalanced to begin with. Repeat the exercise several times until the horse is confident, relaxed and trotting rhyth-

mically over the three poles. Then allow the horse to walk and reward him.

## The first fence

Now set up your first fence - a low cross bar with a placing pole 2.5m (8ft) in front of it. Remember to include a sliding rail to stop the lunge rein getting caught on the fence (as shown in the accompanying photographs); a guide rail on the outside of the fence is a help, especially if lungeing outside. Lunge the horse in the same way as over the trotting poles. It is important that the lunger moves with the horse and doesn't hamper the horse's jump or landing in any way.

As the horse gains confidence in his jumping so the fence can be changed to a vertical rail, or another pole can be placed just behind the cross bar. The fence height is still around 45cms (1ft 6ins). I like to retain a placing pole, but you may have to alter the distance a little depending on how your horse approaches the jump.

Teach the horse to jump from a trot. He must learn to maintain rhythm, balance and control so that he has time to think, assess the situation and be able to use himself correctly over the obstacle.

*6.5 - 6.6  A horse jumping his first cross bar. The lunger encourages the horse forward with voice and whip. He keeps a quiet contact on the lunge rein and goes in the direction of the horse's movement.*

*6.7   A balanced landing. Now is the time to change the fence.*

*6.8   The horse now attempts a small vertical.*

The quality of the jump shown by the horse should always be paramount in your mind, not the height of the fence.

Some horses become quite excited about their jumping and kick and buck after their jump on the lunge. This is fine - up to a point - but it can get out of hand and spoil their jump.

If they become too keen and pull away from you, this should be checked. One way to do this is to use a check rein as described earlier. Allow him to jump the fence and then circle him immediately without permitting him to shoot off, bucking. Make him concentrate and listen to you on the circle. After doing that twice, you should find that the problem is cured.

You can then attach the lunge rein to the cavesson in the usual way and lunge him over the fence again. You should find that he is much more sensible and prepared to concentrate on the work being asked of him.

*6.9 - 6.10   Sometimes horses do get quite excited...*

*...and may kick and buck.*

6.11   *This horse has made a lot of progress during his first jumping exerience. It is now time to stop. Do not be tempted to go higher and higher just because the horse appears willing.*

6.12   *Always reward your horse with kind words and a stroke, even a mouthful of oats!*

6.13   *An experienced horse showing a good bascule with engagement of the knees and fetlocks.*

## Rewarding the horse

Whenever the horse jumps a fence well it is important to reward him. You can do this by saying *'Good boy'* immediately after a good jump, then bring him back to a halt and stroke him on the neck. Giving him a mouthful of oats can be greatly appreciated. You must establish a good rapport with your horse so that he quickly understands what he has to do to please you.

## Varying the jumping work

There is not a lot of point in lungeing a horse routinely over a small fence once or twice a week: he soon learns what is required, gets bored, and puts little effort into his jumping. As a result he becomes careless and uninspired. This is why it is important to keep altering the fence. However, if the horse on his first day jumps well and with ease over a small fence (50-60cm/1ft 6ins-2ft high), it is better to stop at that point rather than to risk frightening the horse by asking for more. Some spooky

6.14  *A horse jumping with a check rein. Note the freedom of rein allowed whilst the horse is over the jump. All corrections must be made either before the approach or after the jump, but not over the jump.*

6.15  *Horses must be taught to jump on both reins. Whenever you change the rein, always start with the fence lower until the horse gains confidence.*

horses may only be able to cope with a small cross bar (50cm/1ft 6ins) on the first day, so don't be tempted to rush forward too soon.

After a few days' training over fences the horse may begin to get a bit casual in his attitude to jumping. This is the time to increase the size to 90cm/3ft and perhaps to alter the look of the fence. A variety of coloured poles, small fillers, a row of upturned plastic buckets, etc. can be utilised to make the jump look different, which will encourage the horse to give you a wonderful jump - he will lower his head when approaching and this will help him to use his back and whole body in a nice bascule.

The jump can be made into a spread fence, first by lowering the height of the vertical to 60cm/2ft and introducing a second pole beyond the vertical. When the horse jumps this new obstacle with confidence, gradually increase the size and width to improve agility.

It is better to set the horse technical problems, through distance variation and fence construction, than to build a higher and wider fence of a few poles. It is always preferable to increase the width rather than the height since this makes the horse

use his brain as well as his body. Do not be tempted to give in to the urge to see the horse jump bigger and bigger.

## General advice on jumping on the lunge

It is important that you jump the horse on both reins. Perhaps on the first day what you achieve on one rein will be sufficient, but after that you should think of changing the rein. When you do this it is important to lower the jump right down as it will look different to the horse and he could easily lose his confidence if he knocks a pole.

After three or four lessons of jumping on the lunge you should be able to assess the horse's potential as a jumper. If he is clumsy and often knocks the jump, and makes little effort to jump bigger after a knock-down, then perhaps he is not going to be a great asset as a jumper! However, do make sure that you, as a handler, are giving the horse the freedom to jump the fence correctly. Horses can sometimes try to land too quickly - thereby restricting their bascule - because they are frightened that the handler will not allow them enough freedom to land and then come round on the circle. This can happen if the handler does not move with the horse when the horse is negotiating the jump.

The other (and ignorant) way to destroy a horse's jump is to whip the horse for knocking down a fence. This makes the horse frightened of the handler so he no longer concentrates on the fence but tries to rush over it to get away from the whip, thus ruining his jump.

Try to put yourself in the horse's position and see things from his point of view. If more people did this, horses would be happier and more confident in their work.

Always remember that if a horse has any trouble with a fence you should immediately reduce the size. If it is a big problem and the horse has lost his confidence, repeat the same (easier) exercise for the next two or three days so that you establish, through repetition, an understanding in the horse's mind of what is required of him. Rest him from jumping for a few days before starting to jump him over bigger fences again and proceed slowly with your increase in height.

A horse who is happy with his jumping comes to the fence with a casual air about him and jumps it with ease. If he makes a mistake and knocks the fence, he will either refuse to jump the fence next time, in which case he may not be bold enough to be a great jumper, or he will come to the fence, look at it and jump with more zest and effort - if so, he is probably a good, bold jumper.

If he has hurt himself and is rather anxious about it, then he will rush at the fence to try to get over it as quickly as possible. This horse is bold but you will have to regain his confidence by making everything easy for him. He will probably make a good jumper, but you must be careful not to proceed too quickly with him. Always remember that a horse who increases his speed when asked to jump is not really confident; he is anxious about something. So look back at what you have done with him. Did you overface him last time you jumped him? Did he hit a fence hard and upset his confidence? Of course, this can easily happen, and, if so, you must reduce the size of the fence

*6.16    A parallel jump is introduced and a second rail placed on the first vertical to make the horse observe the fence. The horse is a little surprised by the second rail and is jumping slightly unbalanced and twisting his shoulders.*

until his confidence is restored.

The horse who refuses to jump should not be written off after one faint-hearted lesson. He should be asked to jump again over a fence which is reduced in size, and may need a flick with the whip to encourage him to go forward to the fence. This will be correct and you may have to ask him to jump the same fence several times before he has the confidence to approach it without assistance from the whip. When this is achieved he should be rewarded and not jumped for a few days. After another two or three jumping lessons you will be able to decide whether he is going to enjoy his jumping or not. There are a few horses who show very little talent at three or four years yet will surprise you with their ability if left for another six or eight months.

I do not approve of jumping foals, yearlings or two-year-olds, except as described at the beginning of the chapter, but a reasonably fit three-year-old should be able to show some ability. It is a known fact that the ends of young horses' bones haven't fully formed until they have a complete mouth at five years, so I don't feel it can be good for them to jump large obstacles and land on their joints until they are five years old or above. I am sure that if you overwork your horse at three or four years you can considerably shorten his working life.

Having got your horse jumping confidently and established that he has a lot of talent, you can progress his training on the lunge so that when he is ridden, grids and doubles hold no surprises. The only thing he has to do is adjust his balance to carry the weight of the rider.

## Grids and doubles

It is quite possible to train horses to jump grids and double jumps on the lunge. The art lies in the lunger, in the confidence he has given his horse and in his ability to set up the jumps correctly. While lungeing, you will need a good assistant on the ground to alter the fences for you. If the horse becomes bored while you are fiddling around putting up the fences he loses respect for you and the fences.

When setting up a grid of two fences, start with a vertical to a vertical and make the distance between the two elements quite short - the horse will be a bit surprised by the second fence and will probably hold back a little. A distance of 2.7m (8ft 9ins.) (2.4m/8ft for ponies) should be about right to start with then, as the horse becomes accustomed to the arrangement, you can increase the height and the distance, depending on the size of the horse and the size of the fence.

The distance can be increased to 2.8m (9ft) and up to 3m (9ft 9ins) (up to around 2.55m/8ft 6ins for ponies). The fence height should be only 45-60cms (1ft 6ins-2ft). If your horse is inclined to rush, keep the distance fairly short, and if he is a

bit lacking in impulsion then move it out a little to encourage him to go forward more actively.

When setting up your grid it is helpful to have a guide rail on the outside of the second fence (see photos), and of course it is still very important to have a sliding rail on both elements to prevent the lunge rein catching on the jump. The grid can be set slightly on a circle if you have an outside guide rail.

If you are going to set up a double fence with a single stride in between, again start with the distance a little shorter than normal. Place the two elements 6m (19ft 6ins) apart (15cm/6ins less for ponies) until the horse is confident and jumping both fences with ease. If you increase the height or width of the fences you must increase the distance accordingly, from about 6.2m (20ft) up to 7m (22ft 9ins) (5.4-6m/18-20ft for ponies).

*6.17   This is a very correct jump over a vertical. The horse shows confidence, a good bascule, and is very well balanced.*

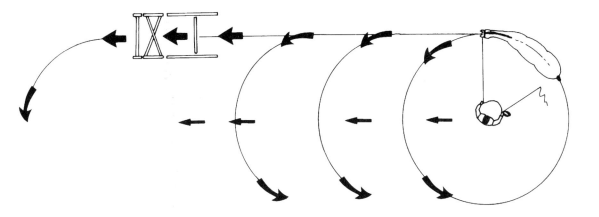

*Fig.12   Jumping on the lunge. First lunge the horse to settle and loosen him, moving gradually towards the fence. When settled, place yourself closer to the fence so that the horse realises where he has to go. Don't for-*
*get to loosen the feel on the lunge rein as the horse approaches the jump so that there is only a very light contact when he is jumping. This allows the horse's head and neck the freedom to make a good bascule.*

As before, if the horse is inclined to rush his fences, keep the distance a little shorter until he is confident and steadies himself.

For the lazy horse the distance can be slightly longer, even up to 8m (26ft) (or 6.3m/21ft for ponies).

The horse will soon discover that he can jump the fences with less effort on his part if he comes in with more impulsion. In this way he learns to think for himself, judge the distances and create his own impulsion, or to steady himself without the interference of the rider.

## Notes for the lunger

The lunger is most important to the horse if this is to be a harmonious training session, and jumping combination fences on the lunge should only be started when the horse is jumping confidently over single fences. The horse must be obedient to the lunger's voice; he should slow down when asked to 'steady' and be keen to go forward with just a click of the tongue.

The lunger must be sure to place himself correctly before the jump so that the horse can be circled until the correct speed within the pace is

achieved. The lunger can then shift his position to indicate to the horse that he is to move towards the fence (see Fig. 12). The lunger must be positive in his movements. Anyone who is diffident about where he should be will upset the horse's confidence and take his mind off what he is doing. This could have disastrous consequences.

With lazy horses it is helpful to have an assistant to carry a whip. If you have to be close enough to use the whip then you haven't enough rein to allow the horse sufficient freedom over the fences. If the whip does have to be used, a sharp flick on the hind leg will encourage him to go forward. If you click with the tongue at the same time, the horse will come to associate the sound of click with the action of whip.

Soon you will be able to dispense with the whip to send him on. He will learn that when he responds correctly by increasing the impulsion not only will he be rewarded by a *'Good boy'* from you but also he will find the jump easier to negotiate.

Working in this way you can establish a very good relationship with the horse, but you must be **positive** about what you are asking him and **quick to reward** him when he has done well. It is also very important that you don't lunge over jumps for too long as horses can quickly become tired and this will spoil their enjoyment of jumping and could harm their legs.

It is important to make jumping enjoyable for the horse, so it should not be practised daily; once or twice a week is ample for a young horse.

## The ideal picture

Anything which is forced cannot be correct. A horse jumping on the lunge should be confident in his handler, have respect, show a sense of rhythm, use his brain, eye up the fence and jump the obstacle in a harmonious balance using his head, neck and back in a beautiful arch. His front legs should fold forward at the elbow and the knees should be fully flexed. The hind legs should flow out behind the horse over the jump.

Jumping on the lunge can be a pleasure for both horse and handler, and the rapport between them should be evident to all who observe them in action.

*6.18  Here the jump is made into an ascending parallel about 15cms/6ins larger than the last jump. The horse is still confident and correct in his outline. Now is the time to reward him.*

# 7. Advanced Long-Reining

Advanced long-reining requires a lot of time, patience and fitness on the part of the handler. The horse must be muscled up and fit as the movements you will be asking him to perform require strength and agility. Moreover he must be very responsive to the forward and sideways driving aids but work with collected steps so that you are not having to run along behind him.

The following exercises assume that the horse has done his elementary long-reining as described in Chapter 4, but if you are starting with an older horse who has not previously been long-reined, then work through all the preliminaries described in that chapter before attempting these more difficult movements.

## Preparing for work and avoiding mishaps

The horse should be saddled or fitted with a roller. The two lunge reins are attached to the bit rings and passed through the stirrups (if saddled) or

*7.2   Always stand to the near side when you first drop the offside rein over the horse's quarters. Note how the rein runs directly from the horse's mouth, through the roller rings to the handler's hand, which must be carried with a bent elbow.*

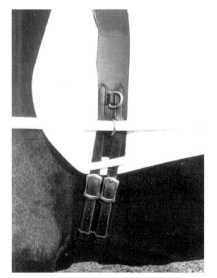

*7.1
Long reins running through a ring on the roller. The rings on the roller are positioned so that the reins are low enough to control the horse's quarters and can run directly to the handler's hand.*

through the rings of the roller (see Photo 7.1).

Always stand to the near side when you first drop the offside rein over the horse's quarters (as shown in Photo 7.2) - some horses can be a little keen and excited so never take any silly chances. I cannot stress too strongly that **you must be at a safe distance behind the horse** and only get closer to him if you can fully trust him. In fact, I never entirely trust a horse, even a trained one, and always move back when asking for canter or the first flying changes. It is also important that you never lose your concentration, as this can easily court disaster. If you do have the misfortune to be kicked at by a horse then he must be corrected immediately with a good slap from both reins and a scolding voice: he must be halted and stood so that he has a few moments to think about his misdemeanours. Afterwards continue with whatever it was you were doing.

## Cantering on a circle

Start in walk on a circle, then trot on the circle so that the horse gets used to the feel of the reins around his quarters. When the horse is settled and listening to you on the circle, change the rein several times. If you feel the horse is ready, he can be asked to canter on the circle. As this will be his first long-rein canter aid it is important that you

have the correct feel on the reins. Ask the horse to canter with your voice (saying 'Can-ter'), keep a quiet but steady feel on the inside rein and quietly but firmly flick the outside rein round his quarters. Try to use the outside rein in a stroking movement, much as you would your leg when giving a ridden aid to canter. If he does not respond, collect the horse again with a little flap of the reins and a click with your tongue, and apply a little restraint on the reins. This will 'compress' the horse. Now repeat the canter aid. You could carry a whip in your outside hand but I very rarely use one - the horse usually responds to the voice. Of course, when the horse answers the aid to canter, reward him with your voice.

The canter will, at this stage, be too fast for you to long-rein behind him, so you must teach the horse to collect the canter on the circle. Firstly, you must establish the canter transition from trot to canter on both reins as described above. Next ask the horse to go from walk to canter in the same way. As the horse canters on the circle, try to collect him. He must be taught to be responsive to the rein aids in both trot and canter. He must not be allowed to lean on the reins, which is what he will start to do as you drive him up to them. If he gets too strong, stop him, lighten the contact and either trot or canter again. You may have to repeat this exercise many times on both reins until the horse is light and listening to you. This can take

7.3 - 7.5   (Right to left) The rein-back, here used to control the horse. The horse's ears show that he is listening. The neck is a little tense at the beginning of the sequence, but by the third picture the horse is softening and relaxing. The steps are in diagonal pairs.

several days' training but it is most important that you get the horse to listen to you before you progress further.

Sometimes, with big, strong horses I find that walking on a straight line and working through the walk-halt-walk transitions is a good way to start. If the horse is still rather strong in the reins then take him on a circle and work him in all the transitions. Make the downward transitions come fairly quickly and the upward transitions come more slowly. When you have the upward pace then stay in that pace for just a short time so that the horse does not get too much power in the steps. For example, trot for a quarter of a circle, then walk, canter for a quarter of a circle, then walk, etc. until the horse is waiting for the downward transition. Now you should be able to drive him forward in the pace you require, with the horse remaining light on the reins.

## The rein-back

In the rein-back the horse is pushed up with both reins gently stroking his sides, but then restrained and asked with the voice, saying 'Back'. As the horse cannot step forward he has to step back (see Photos 7.3-7.5). As soon as he does step back, lighten the reins a little and say 'Good boy'. Repeat for a few more steps. I like to stop the horse reining

back with the voice, saying 'Whoa' or 'Walk on', or just 'Good boy' if he has responded well.

In the rein-back it is important not to hurry the forward move-off. Often I find it helpful to halt the horse, move forward to the side of the horse and stroke him on the quarters before repositioning myself and continuing in walk.

You must be sure that the horse does not anticipate the rein-back and that he will always halt up to the bit and not step back until asked to do so. If he does step back as soon as he halts, then it may be better to move him forward into trot and do some trot-walk-trot transitions before coming back to halt again. Practise the halt and forward transition again without halting for long so that the horse is thinking forward and up to the bit. When the halt is well established then the rein-back can be attempted again. It is better to ask only for a few steps at first and make sure that the horse is on the aids before asking for more regular steps back.

When the rein-back is established, try the following exercise: halt, rein-back six steps, walk forward six steps, rein-back four steps, go forward into walk again. Practise until the last three transitions are performed without a pause. This is a very good exercise in obedience and also helps to adjust the horse's balance. The handler must, however, be sure that his hands are light, soft and responsive to the feeling of the horse, and he must follow the movement smoothly.

## Canter transitions

The canter transitions must now be perfected. Having established walk to canter on the circle, it is time for you to train the horse to repeat the exercise with you directly behind him. You may, to start with, have to run behind the horse until he is collected enough to canter at a speed you can match at a fast walk.

The first transition is most easily attempted when walking the horse towards the first corner of the short side of the arena. You then have the short side for collected canter and can either turn the horse soon after the short side, or if he is getting too fast or too strong, you can ask for a downward transition again to walk. Repeat this exercise several times until the upward transition is established in the horse's mind. Then repeat it on the other rein. When the transitions to canter are obeyed, a six-loop serpentine in canter (his assumes a 20 x 60m arena), with simple changes across the centre line, is a good progression. If you can perform this movement smoothly, reward the horse with short breaks of walk. Remember, the work is nearly as hard for him as it is for you!

Having established the canter aid you have the basis for teaching the flying change in the future, but before proceeding to this next stage in canter I feel it important to perfect the sideways aids and to establish shoulder-in and half-pass in trot so that you can easily progress to these movements in canter.

## Shoulder-in

The technique for shoulder-in was discussed in Chapter 4; however, the horse may benefit from a refresher course on the aids. Remind him of the shoulder-in at walk. As you come out of a corner, push the horse with a light flap of the inside rein into a firmer, steady feel on the outside rein and place his shoulder in with a little feel on the inside rein (Photos 7.6-7.7). The inside rein should be light and gently stroking his side to keep him soft and bent to the inside. If the horse tries to turn

*7.6  Shoulder-in. As you come out of the corner, push the horse with a light flap of the inside rein into a firmer, steadier feel of the outside rein and place his shoulder in with a little feel of the inside rein.*

across the school or come off the track then he must be taken back to the track with the outside rein. This can then be lightened slightly and the horse asked to bend again with a little inside rein.

The horse will soon learn that he has to accept a constant light feel of the outside rein and listen to the light stroking movement of the inside rein. The horse must be firmly established in this movement before proceeding with other movements. Practise the shoulder-in in different places so that the horse responds quickly and easily, whether from a straight line, a corner or out of a circle.

## Travers

It is now time to teach the horse travers or quarters-in. This is not usually very difficult for the

*7.7 Shoulder-in. The horse will soon learn to accept the constant light feel on the outside rein and that he must listen to the light stroking movement of the inside rein.*

*7.8 Travers. Here the horse is bent to the right with the inside rein, and the outside rein is flapping to bring his quarters in from the track.*

horse to grasp as it is a follow-on from the shoulder-in.

The rein aids are: inside rein, which is constant and keeps the bend to the inside, and outside rein, which gently strokes the quarters inwards (Photo 7.8). The outside rein is still constant but the hindquarters are brought to the inside of the track by small half-halts, while you walk on the inside track. If the horse does not respond and yield his quarters to the inside then you may have to move the outside rein a bit, but you should not have to flap it against his side as this would be too much like the canter strike-off aid. If he does not respond at all, you will have to slap his outside with the rein to move the quarters in, then as he moves them let the rein lie constantly against his side so that he yields his quarters to the inside while you keep the inside bend with a light inside rein.

Of course, as soon as the horse answers in the correct way he must be rewarded with a *'Good boy'* and a lightening of the reins.

Again, this movement must be established in the horse's mind before proceeding to other movements. Make sure that you can move from shoulder-in to travers, perhaps by making a small circle out of shoulder-in and then moving into travers as you come out of the circle. You must be able to perform these two movements down the side of the school, on the centre line or away from the track so that you are in complete control of the shoulders and quarters.

## The half-pirouette

The half-pirouette is a natural progression from shoulder-in and travers in the walk pace. The horse walks a small half-turn, with the front legs stepping sideways around the hind legs, and the hind legs keeping the walk sequence staying nearly on the same spot. The horse is bent in the direction of the movement.

At first, of course, keep the movement large until the horse understands what is being asked of him and is able to collect his steps so that they are small and neat for a correct pirouette. Start by

walking in a straight line then collect the steps with small half-halts. Gently push him into a slight shoulder-in, and when you want to make the pirouette, turn him with the inside rein but make little half-halts with the outside rein to stop the quarters moving out. You have to contain the energy with the outside rein and gently turn and then release the horse in the direction you wish him to move.

## Half-pass and renvers

Having successfully performed the half-pirouette, your horse is set up to do a half-pass. All you need to do is keep the bend and push him sideways with the outside rein giving little half-halts, and this will encourage him to step in half-pass back to the track.

The half-pass is a movement where the horse moves forward and sideways with his body bent in the direction in which he his moving (Photos 7.9-

7.13). In the half-pass it is important to be able to keep the bend as well as the forwards and side-ways steps. It is easy to fall into the trap of allowing the horse to drop onto the inside shoulder and to run sideways. This must not be permitted, so correct the horse by driving him forward with the inside rein and ask again for the correct bend.

In the half-pass it is important that the handler moves sideways quickly enough and does not get left behind the movement, thereby causing the quarters to trail. If the quarters do lag behind, make a half-halt with the outside rein to straighten the horse and then continue with the correct bend in the direction of movement, and contain the sideways movement with the outside rein firmly pressing against the horse's side. This movement can be performed in all three paces; Photo 7.14 shows a canter half-pass.

There is a tendency for horses not to finish the half-pass, especially if they are in an indoor arena, where they tend to lose the bend before they arrive at the track. This can be corrected by performing a

*7.9 - 7.11   Half-pass left. The horse is bent to the left with the left rein. The handler contains the quarters with the right rein round the quarters and pushes the horse sideways with the right rein. The handler needs to be to the left of the quarters when executing a left half-pass.*

*7.12 - 7.13   (Below) Here the horse is performing a good half-pass to the left.*

7.14   *Correct canter half-pass left.*

7.15   *If the quarters are inclined to trail in half-pass, the handler should move quickly to the side and continue in renvers, as shown here.*

**renvers** movement (Photos 7.15-7.17). This is very like a half-pass but instead the horse moves in a straight line.

In this movement the horse's quarters are on the track, his shoulders are in from the track and he is bent in the direction of travel. The aids for renvers are the same as those for half-pass, and indeed renvers is often performed out of the half-pass. So, when you are nearing the track in half-pass, steady the sideways steps by half-halting with the outside rein, but continue to push the quarters sideways to the track and then keep the bend with the inside rein. The inside rein is now on the outside of the arena, but is considered the inside rein as it is the bending rein, not the balancing rein. It remains the inside rein until you move out of this movement by allowing the horse to put his shoulders back on a straight line, then it can be described as the outside rein again.

## Canter flying changes

In the canter flying change the horse jumps from one canter stride to the other and lands on the other lead. This is one of the most difficult movements to teach the horse in long reins and also the most dangerous for the handler - it is the time when the horse is most likely to kick.

If you have reached this stage you will already have established canter and simple changes with the horse (as described earlier in this chapter), but it would be wise to refresh his memory and do several upward and downward transitions from walk to canter right and walk to canter left, until he is thinking of changing on to the other leg.

When he is confident and settled in his mind, work him in a serpentine figure and instead of doing a simple change ask for a flying change. This is done by lightening your outside rein and gently

7.16   Renvers. Asking for more right bend with the right rein while containing the quarters with the left rein to complete the bend.

7.17   Renvers. Correct bend through the horse's body and neck. A happy, active picture.

re-taking it as you ask for the flying change, then change into the new direction. The 'old' inside rein is then stroked against his side as you take up the firmer contact. To start with you may have to slap the rein against his side to encourage him to change legs, and I always give a little click with my tongue to invite more energy. See Photos 7.18-7.20.

If the horse does change legs, reward him with the voice or stop and pat him. If he doesn't understand what you want, go back to walk before trying again. If he makes only one change, or if he changes only his front legs, reward him nevertheless as he has made a start. Don't go on asking for too long. It is far better to attempt the exercise over several short bouts than to try to achieve your goal in one long session from which you both emerge hot and bothered.

With a horse who repeatedly doesn't change correctly, take him onto a circle until he changes behind, then reward him with a walk.

Once the horse understands what is required of him he becomes very responsive to the change-of-leg aid. Most horses seem really to enjoy doing flying changes, and in some cases it is difficult to stop them! In fact, flying changes can be used as an evasion for avoiding other movements, so if the horse gives you flying changes instead of what you are asking of him, take care. This is one time when he could kick out in excitement as he is not totally under control.

At first you should be fairly satisfied if the horse makes any attempt to change legs and you should praise him with your voice. However, when he does a *correct* flying change, reward him with your voice and a halt, stroke him on the neck and finish for the day. If you do this for a few days he will soon realise what is required.

## Canter half-pass with flying changes

When you can perform a six-loop serpentine with flying changes on the centre line, the horse is ready to start being asked to do them in other parts of the arena. He will also be ready to do canter half-passes (Photos 7.21-7.24) incorporating flying changes for changes of direction.

Here you must pay attention to keeping the bend in the direction of travel, then allow the horse to go straight for a few steps before asking for a flying change. It is very important at the beginning to keep every movement separate so that the horse has time to concentrate on what is being asked of him. He will then perform the movements correctly and without tension. Do one

7.18 - 7.20 (Right to left) Canter flying changes. Start by working on a serpentine and ask for a change as you cross the centre line. Change the bend and stroke the horse's side with the new outside rein.

canter half-pass and a flying change, then walk and reward him. Take up canter again and do the same thing on the other rein. When this is perfected you can perform, say, a half-pass to the right, then a flying change to the left and immediately a half-pass to the left.

A few days of training are needed to master these movements but when they are polished you

7.21 - 7.24 Canter half-pass. The horse is correctly bent in left canter.

7.25 - 7.29
(Clockwise from bottom right)
Canter pirouette right.

can try a zig-zag half-pass. In this movement the horse half-passes for a number of steps, first one way and then the other, making a flying change between each change of direction. Performed well this looks most impressive, but the handler must be careful to keep the half-pass under control and to steady the sideways steps before asking for the flying change. The handler needs to allow the horse to go straight for the change step, then must compress him sideways with the outside rein whilst keeping the bend and pushing him forward with the inside rein.

## Canter pirouettes

The horse is now ready to perform canter pirouettes (Photos 7.25-7.29). In this movement the horse canters a very small circle with the hind legs nearly on the same spot, keeping the rhythm of the canter steps; the forehand, working in rhythm, makes a larger circle and the horse is bent throughout in the direction of the movement. The aids are the same as for the half-pass but the horse is asked for maximum collection and performs the half-pass on the circle. The handler needs to position himself much nearer to the horse in order to perform this movement to perfection, so it can only be carried out if you can trust your horse completely. (See Photos 7.30-7.32 for clarification of where to stand.)

The horse needs to be pretty fit to perform this movement as most of his weight has to be carried on his hind legs. It can be a strain on him if he is asked to do too much.

The pirouette can be started from the circle or when cantering on a straight line or from the half-pass. The horse is asked to collect the steps then turn a few steps, keeping the bend with the inside rein and controlling the quarters with the outside rein held firmly round his quarters. Care must be taken to allow the movement while still controlling the quarters.

When a half-pirouette is performed successfully then a whole pirouette can be worked on. As the horse becomes increasingly more collected, the pirouette will become smaller.

Sometimes a horse will try to drop the contact on the inside rein and will suddenly turn in and lose the bend. This must be quickly corrected by using the inside rein to drive the horse out so that he doesn't drop the contact on the inside rein. The outside rein keeps the balance. Make the horse go forward onto a much larger circle while keeping the bend in the direction of the movement, make the circle a little smaller for a few steps then go out on a larger circle again until the horse is really obedient and listening to you. Really small pirouettes should be performed only occasionally, but the larger pirouettes can be worked on more often to prepare the horse for the correct movement.

The inside rein has two roles in the pirouette: one asking for the bend, and the other keeping the horse moving forward, being used in a light stroking manner.

When teaching the horse the pirouette it is important that you are always able to move out easily onto a straight line. You must keep testing the horse to make sure that he is fully on the aids. Asking him for a few steps of pirouette and moving out is an easy lesson to start with, then try a half pirouette. Later, when the horse is very collected and well balanced, you can make a whole pirouette or even a double one.

Try to be aware that the horse has to work out for himself how to make smaller steps with his hind legs while performing larger ones with his forelegs. A big-striding horse can find this quite difficult.

It is sensible to keep the flying-change work quite separate from teaching the pirouette. Some people make the mistake of asking for some pirouette steps then performing a flying change a few strides afterwards. This is inclined to make the horse anticipate the change, so he becomes excited in the pirouette and changes his hind legs, thereby becoming disunited.

Correctly executed, the pirouette is a very beautiful movement; it is the most collected movement in the canter pace, therefore be careful not to over-exert your horse when teaching him this exercise. It is somewhat easier for the handler as

*7.30 - 7.32   (Anti-clockwise from above) Canter pirouette left. These pictures indicate the rein aids and position of the handler for a small pirouette.*

you don't have to move so far or so fast! Remember, the horse is extremely collected and using all his muscles and tendons from the tip of his hind feet through his back to his mouth, and you should respect the degree of effort involved.

## Tempi flying changes

In tempi flying changes the horse jumps from one canter stride to the other with a set number of normal strides between each change of leg. In four-time changes the horse makes a flying change followed by three canter strides, then another change and so on. The strides in between can be reduced until the horse is jumping from one leading leg to the other, like a child skipping along the road; these are called one-time changes. When the horse has learned tempi changes it is easier to do one-time changes than two- or three-time changes.

Tempi changes are another movement where it could be extremely easy for you to get kicked, so beware and don't take any silly chances - every horse can get over-excited.

In flying changes the horse must be responsive and not take too much contact on the rein. It is easier to be accurate when the horse is having to be pushed forward a little than when he is too strong, which is why I have put these movements here, after the pirouettes. The pirouettes will make the horse more collected and lighter in the forehand, so therefore the changes will be easier for him.

When teaching the tempi changes it is easier to start on the diagonal or away from the side of the arena, off the track. Once positioned on the line you are to take, it is important that you get the horse to do the changes straight and without deviating from that line. Ask for the first change in the normal way - by lightening your 'old' inside rein, taking a more constant feel on the old outside rein as you stroke the horse's side with the 'old' inside rein and allowing the change to go through by not restricting the movement in any way. In the beginning the horse will probably increase his speed slightly. This is normal. When the horse has responded to two or three changes on the straight line, walk and praise him. When you are ready, take up canter again and repeat until you can get the changes when you ask for them on the straight line. (See Photos 7.33-7.34) I find it helpful to give a little click with the tongue when asking for the change as it makes the horse listen to you a little more.

With long reins it is not so easy to be as accurate with your aids as when you are riding the horse as you are so far away from him. Three-time and two-time changes are not very difficult to develop from the four-times, but if you are a bit late in giving the aid then you tend to make the horse go faster and faster. If this happens you must speed up your aids by a fraction and when the horse performs a few tempi changes correctly reward him with a walk and stroke him on the neck. It is much better to ask for just a few tempi changes and get them right than to ask for a long line of them and make mistakes as neither of you learns anything that way.

The one-time changes are asked for by quick strokes with the rein on either side of the horse's quarters. As soon as he responds with a few cor-

*7.33 - 7.34  Flying changes on the straight line can take a lot of patience and timing on the part of the handler.*

*The pictures below show right and left flying changes.*

rect steps, reward him. I find it better not to repeat the one-time changes too often on one day. They come very easily in a few days' training, and once the horse knows what is wanted of him I find that if you keep the rein close to his sides and click with your tongue in time to the movement, he will perform them willingly. In fact, horses really enjoy doing this movement, and most would rather do the one-times rather than the twos or the threes.

Once you have established the one-tempi changes, you will find that you have to work on the horse's obedience in the other changes. The more time and patience you can spend on the twos, threes and fours, the better. The horse will often keep trying to give you one-time changes when you are asking for twos or threes. In this case turn him and put him onto a normal canter stride, giving a small correction with the outside rein and a scold with your voice.

If the horse offers changes when they are not required it is a help to work on shallow serpentine loops until the horse is obedient to the aid again. You can then go back to doing the changes on a straight line, but always remember that the fault may lie with you. Your timing of the change aid could be too early for the horse, therefore causing confusion. Keep double-checking your own technique before you accuse the horse.

# 8. Piaffe and Passage

## Piaffe on the short hand rein

The piaffe is the most collected of the trot paces. The horse shows an elevated and cadenced trot on the spot, with the quarters slightly lowered. He should demonstrate great freedom and mobility of all the joints as he moves each diagonal pair of legs. The toe of each foreleg should be raised to halfway up the cannon bone; and the hind legs, showing great activity, should lift each hind toe to just above the hind fetlock joint. The horse must always have the desire to move forward and show a lively impulsion, whilst remaining lightly on the bit.

Working a horse on what we call a short hand rein is one of the ways of teaching the early steps of piaffe without the weight of the rider on his back. This work is also useful in teaching the horse the correct reaction to the whip.

The equipment required is a cavesson, snaffle bridle, saddle or roller, elasticated side-reins, two lunge reins, front boots, and a whip with a short lash. You will also need an assistant - and some chopped carrots to offer the horse as a reward.

To start this work the horse must be practised in the early training and able to accept the side-reins readily and with confidence when standing and walking. The horse should lead forward easily when asked and understand the voice aids. The assistant should be acquainted with the horse and should lead him forward and ask him to halt a few times (using a lunge rein attached to the central ring on the cavesson). The next step is for the trainer to attach a second lunge rein to the offside ring of the cavesson (see Photo 8.1). This rein goes over the withers to the trainer, who stands level with the

hindquarters on the near side (as shown). The offside rein helps to prevent the horse turning his quarters away from the trainer or pushing past the assistant. With the side-reins attached, the horse is placed on the track with the assistant standing on the near side, by the horse's shoulder but facing

*8.1   This horse is tacked up ready for short hand work. Note the second lunge rein attached to the offside ring of the cavesson. This rein goes over the withers to the trainer, who stands near the near-side hindquarters.*

8.2
The horse must be taught to raise each hind leg when touched with the whip. He must learn to raise it and move it forward.

To start with, the horse must be taught to raise each hind leg when it is touched with the whip (Photo 8.2). He must learn to lift the leg and move it forward, not lift it and push it out behind him. This is something you must quietly insist on until the horse places his leg more underneath his body.

Some horses will kick at the whip, but most can be trained to accept it and to react correctly to a *light* touch. If the horse does react violently, reprimand him with your voice and use the whip a little more sharply. However, common sense must be applied in deciding when to correct a horse. Some thoroughbreds, being bred to compete and to win, are sometimes unsuitable for this training. They must be taught another way, but I have found this necessary only once - and that was with a very difficult horse who had passed through many hands.

The trainer must take care not to upset the horse with the whip. Used correctly, with a light tap on the back of the hind leg, the horse will soon learn to react in the right way. As soon as the horse lifts his leg he must be rewarded by the assistant with a stroke on the neck and a praising *'Good boy'*.

When you touch the horse with the whip it is a good idea simultaneously to click with your tongue to indicate to the horse that activity is required. As the horse learns to lift both hind legs

backwards and able to move backwards when necessary. In this position the assistant can observe the horse's reactions, and can help with the next step in the training.

The side-reins have to be fairly tight here as the horse becomes more collected, but common sense must be used. It is always safer to begin with the side-reins too long and shorten them, than to have them too short at the outset.

8.3   This horse is reacting calmly to the whip, yet this is the first time that she has been introduced to this technique. The assistant must allow her to move forward.

8.4   The mare is beginning to take diagonal steps, though the foreleg has not been lifted high enough to make a true step. It is a good attempt for a first timer...

*8.5    ...at this point reward the horse and finish. Note the correct halt.*

*8.7    If the horse is restricted or held tightly in any way, a resistance such as rearing or running backwards can be caused. Both should be avoided, but misunderstandings do happen; always try to finish on a happy note.*

at the touch of the whip, you can ask the assistant to lead him forward with short walk steps. At a suitable moment the trainer can ask for two short piaffe steps, giving two little taps with the whip accompanied by vocal clicks. To start with, the horse may be a bit slow to react. If so, the assistant

can move the horse forward until he shows some short trot steps, then the trainer can ask for more activity in the steps with light taps. As soon as the horse shows increased activity with the hind legs,

*8.6    Piaffe in the short hand rein. The horse is showing some very active steps. It is essential to allow him to move forward, or the diagonal steps will get too close under the horse and upset the balance. The right foreleg is angled backwards too much.*

*8.8    The leader has allowed the horse more freedom, and the whole picture of this piaffe is more relaxed. Now is the time for reward - the side-reins can be removed and the horse quietly walked until he is cooled and settled.*

reward him with the carrots and make a fuss of him. In Photo 8.3 you can see that the horse is beginning to understand what is required of him. Gradually the horse produces a diagonal step, which is only just starting to show in Photo 8.4. As always, praise the horse as soon as any slight improvement is shown (Photo 8.5). It is important to train only for a short time in piaffe. Practising 'little and often' is much better than prolonging the training sessions.

After a few days' training in this way you will be able to dispense with the assistant and second rein. Now you can take up a position of standing by the shoulder. First tap the hind legs as you did on day one, and the horse will know that you are working on the same lines as previously. As soon as he reacts correctly to the whip, reward him and lead him forward. As you walk him forward, you too must turn to face forward. If you do this the horse will soon learn that when you face forward he walks with you and relaxes; and when you turn to face the rear it means that activity is required. As you turn, give him little vibrations on the lunge rein (half-halts) as you activate the hind legs. Reward him as soon as a good reaction is shown. It will not take him long to learn that this pleases you and he will give you his best.

When the horse becomes active and is working well, it is important that you are able to make the horse move forward in piaffe steps and then short-en them so that gradually he is able to perform the movement correctly on the spot - but this must come **gradually**. If it is hurried or overdone, the horse's legs will become tired and he will either run backward or leap forward into the air to escape from the task. This can happen for other reasons, such as when the horse is too fresh or over-excited, and although he should be corrected it should be only a very light correction. If he constantly tries these evasions you can be more severe, but common sense and judgment as to why the evasion has happened are very important. If you feel you have slightly overdone something, walk and gradually return to asking for a few steps of piaffe, then stop.

When the session is over always reward your horse with some carrots or a titbit, undo the side-reins and lead him around quietly until he is cool and settled, with a light rug over his back. After about seven days of work like this I leave the piaffe training for a week or two and then return to it, taking up where I left off. Often the horse comes back to it with renewed vigour and enthusiasm, and if he does, praise him well. I find that the horse soon learns that a click with the tongue and you facing the rear means piaffe and he will usually offer lovely piaffe steps without the use of the whip at all. Of course, that is what you really want - the horse working to please you and not working because of you.

# Piaffe in the long reins

The other way to teach the horse piaffe is in long reins. Here you are directly behind him. This method works quite well with the more exuberant horse, but if he is a rather lazy type you may have to drive him very hard to get a reaction and this will mean that you disturb his mouth, which could upset him. If this is the case you can either have an assistant walking beside him with a whip, or you could carry one yourself, which I feel is preferable.

Throughout this work, you must take great care that you don't get kicked. Obviously, any horse who is not fully confident in what he is being asked is more likely to react against you. Some will kick out and others will run backwards. If the horse does kick, a short reprimand with the voice is probably sufficient. If he runs backwards it could be that your hands are too hard and he feels restricted. In this case, take him back to where you started from and, having lightened the rein tension, ask an assistant to lead the horse for a while until he understands what is required.

Start by asking him to lengthen and shorten his trot steps. First, position yourself directly behind the horse and shorten the trot steps with little half-halting aids, i.e. lightly flapping both reins or giving a light flick with the whip. This will push the horse up to the rein but slightly restrain him until he shortens his trot steps quite considerably.

*8.12 Teaching piaffe in long reins. This horse is on his forehand and taking too strong a contact on the reins. A stick and the voice are used to activate the hind legs.*

At the same time click with your tongue to indicate more energy. To begin with you will only achieve shorter trot steps, but if you ask for a little more every day you will soon have the horse in a true piaffe.

It is important that you always encourage the horse to trot forward again as soon as he has shown some good collected steps. The horse must be on the bit throughout, and therefore needs a light contact on the reins. The movement must be forward so that when the horse offers some good steps you can reward him with a *'Good boy'* with your voice and an allowing rein to let him trot

*8.9 - 8.11 Piaffe in the long reins. Even with a trained horse it is important to allow the piaffe steps to move slightly forward. This horse's steps are very good, with the horse's weight balanced on lowered hindquarters. Ideally the head and neck could be a little lower.*

8.13   *Shortening the trot steps while teaching piaffe in long reins. Note that the reins are in the left hand. The handler is slightly to the right of the hind leg (in case the horse should kick) and a stick is carried in the right hand to touch the hind leg if necessary. This horse is showing good activity, so the stick has not been used.*

8.14   *The same horse (a six-year-old) learning piaffe in long reins, and the horse showing good, active steps. The horse is listening to the handler but is a little tight in the neck. But this is still the time for reward. Always allow the horse to move forward a little with each step.*

forward again.

This method is often useful for a highly couraged horse if you are not able to train him mounted. In this way the horse doesn't feel so restricted and because you are already in the trot pace he can keep a better rhythm in the piaffe steps. I have had good results in training different horses in both ways. The secret is never to work in this movement for too long. If you do the piaffe yourself for one and half minutes you will soon realise how the horse feels if you overdo the work, and the same applies to the passage steps.

## Passage

The passage is a very collected, very elevated, cadenced trot. The horse shows graceful, springy steps with a prolonged moment of suspension. The knees and hocks are highly flexed as the quarters are more engaged and the horse remains lightly on the bit. When this movement is established the horse should then be able to move smoothly from piaffe to passage and back to piaffe without any apparent effort, loss of rhythm or cadence.

When teaching passage it is important that the

horse has established the piaffe steps in his mind and will readily take up piaffe in the long reins. It doesn't seem to matter how the horse has been trained to piaffe; horses who have been trained in the short hand rein seem to take straight away to the long-rein aids, with just a couple of clicks with the tongue and a few light flaps with both reins used alternately as each hind leg is about to leave

8.15   *Passage in long reins.*

*8.16 - 8.21 (Left to right) Passage-piaffe-passage transitions. This horse shows the shortening of the steps well; the activity and understanding are good. It is only with quiet practice that you can work on perfecting this movement, but it must not be performed for too long, as the horse will tire.*

the ground. The horse should immediately start making piaffe steps, and if he does so, halt and reward him.

For passage training you have to push the horse forward in piaffe and give him the feeling in the reins that he has the freedom to make a longer step. It is almost as if you are pushing him but still keeping a balancing hold on the rein. Most difficulties arise when the horse is not allowed to go forward enough and he becomes confused and makes canter or short jumping steps. At this moment say 'Trot' to the horse until he gets a trot rhythm again. Gradually, with quiet encouragement, the horse will pick up the rhythm and balance of the steps. After a few good attempts halt and reward the horse; allow him to relax and take him back to his stable.

After a few days of working at the passage the horse will be able to keep the steps for much longer. If he is breaking backwards and not maintaining the steps then it is highly likely that you are restricting him too much: your hands are too hard and he is frightened of taking forward steps. In this case you must push him strongly forward, even into a trot, and allow with a softer hand. Gradually with both reins push him into the higher, shorter steps of the passage as described above.

If the horse throws his head up as you use the reins to push him forward, then he is worried in his mouth. Cease using the reins for the forward push and resort to a long whip to help create the necessary impulsion. With the whip touch the horse on one hind leg in the rhythm of the step he is to create, while still keeping him balanced with a steady contact on his mouth. As soon as he responds, reward him. It is very important to use tongue clicks in time with the touch of the whip, but when the horse picks up the steps, cease with the voice and gradually push him up with the reins. If he slackens his steps then use voice and whip again until he learns to stay in the movement until asked to stop.

When the passage is fully established in the horse's mind you can increase the activity of the steps with little reminders from the pushing aids of the reins or a touch with the whip if necessary. Allow the horse to move more forward in the passage and to shorten the step in the passage as well. This is a very good exercise to prepare the horse for the transitions of piaffe-passage-piaffe.

## Piaffe-passage transitions

The piaffe-passage transitions are the ultimate in collection, balance and suppleness of the horse. Here the handler must be sure that he never gets behind the movement, especially when moving forward from piaffe to passage, as this will upset the horse and encourage him to hollow his outline and lose his rhythm.

When asking for the transition from passage to piaffe, first shorten the passage steps gradually and then keep the impulsion with your voice (tongue clicks) and a steady, light contact to prevent the horse from moving forward in the piaffe. If impulsion is lacking then energise the horse with alternate slaps of the rein as each hind leg is about to leave the ground. When the horse has performed the required number of steps (five to start with, increasing to fifteen when established) then allow him forward into passage with a lighter rein contact and a click with the tongue, and hold the reins close to his sides so that he gets used to the feel of the rein around him for the transition movement. Over a period of time these transitions must be practised until the horse moves from piaffe to passage without any alteration of rhythm, cadence, balance or outline. When this is achieved you have reached perfection in your training, as well as harmony and trust between yourself and that very noble beast, the horse.

# Conclusion

Training horses is a fascinating and very rewarding art. There are many ways of training but all should produce the same result - a horse that is confident, keen and happy in his work. Anything which is forced or which induces fear is wrong, and it is important for all trainers constantly to reflect on their teaching methods, especially if training sessions are becoming unpleasant, tedious or ragged. We are all lazy and some horses are lazy too. Like us, they may need a sharp correction occasionally, but that should be all. The rapport between horse and trainer can be wonderful - when the horse works to please his master, is confident in what he is doing, is frequently rewarded and never asked to do too much. If trained this way, the horse will become your respected friend and will try to help you with all his power.

# Index